Inspired

2009 Poetry Collection

Inspired represents our student authors as accurately as possible.
Every effort has been made to print each poem
as it was submitted with minimal editing
of spelling, grammar, and punctuation.
All submissions have been formatted to this compilation.

Published by
The America Library of Poetry
P.O. Box 978
Houlton, ME 04730
Website: www.libraryofpoetry.com
Email: generalinquiries@libraryofpoetry.com

Printed in the United States of America.

THE AMERICA
LIBRARY OF POETRY

ISBN-10   0-9773662-4-3
ISBN-13   978-0-9773662-4-8

Contents

Poetry by Division

Inspired

... In memory of Veronica James

When I Get There
by Veronica James

When I get there, I hope it's like they said it'll be
No pain, drama, or stress on me
When I get there, I hope the angels sing
When I get there, I hope there's no rain
When I get there, I hope the clouds are sky blue and white
When I get there, I hope the sun is big and bright
When I get to Heaven, I wish, I want to re-live a different life
Because the pain, tears, and fear will be gone
My heart will be made over, heartbreak free and pain free
When I get to Heaven, I know everything is going to be easy
Praise God that I am officially working for Him
And God knows that all my suffering will soon end
I want to experience new things and have a brand new song to sing
When I look up in the sky, sometimes and smile, I know why
Once I think on my past, I came a long way and more to go
When I think about God, I know He's the right one to know
When I get there and it's all said and done
When I get there and go through Judgment Day
I will remember my past and all the bad I've done
So before I get there, I'm gonna turn my life around
So when I get there, I won't have anything holding me back

Foreword

There are two kinds of writers in the world.
There are those who write from experience,
and those who write from imagination.
The experienced, offer words that are a reflection of their lives.
The triumphs they have enjoyed, the heartaches they have endured;
all the things that have made them who they are,
they graciously share with us, as a way of sharing themselves,
and in doing so, give us, as readers, someone to whom we may relate,
as well as fresh new perspectives
on what may be our common circumstances in life.
From the imaginative,
come all the wonderful things we have yet to experience;
from sights unseen, to sounds unheard.
They encourage us to explore the limitless possibilities
of our dreams and fantasies,
and aid us in escaping, if only temporarily,
the confines of reality and the rules of society.
To each, we owe a debt of gratitude;
and rightfully so, as each provides a service of equal importance.
Yet, without the other, neither can be truly beneficial.
For instance, one may succeed in accumulating a lifetime of experience,
only to consider it all to have been predictable and unfulfilling,
if denied the chance to chase a dream or two along the way.
Just as those whose imaginations run away with them never to return,
may find that without solid footing in the real world,
life in fantasyland is empty.
As you now embark, dear reader,
upon your journey through these inspired words,
you are about to be treated to both heartfelt tales of experience,
and captivating adventures of imagination.
It is our pleasure to present them for your enjoyment.
To our many authors,
who so proudly represent the two kinds of writers in the world,
we dedicate this book, and offer our sincere thanks;
for now, possibly more than ever,
the world needs you both.

Paul Wilson Charles
Editor

Editor's Choice Award

The Editor's Choice Award is presented
to an author who demonstrates not only
the solid fundamentals of creative writing,
but also the ability to illicit an emotional response
or provide a thought provoking body of work
in a manner which is both clear and concise.

You will find "Void and Cracked"
by Danielle Shpaner
on page 217 of *Inspired*

2009
Spirit of Education

For Outstanding Participation

Farmingville
Elementary
School

Ridgefield, Connecticut

Presented to participating students and faculty
in recognition of your commitment
to literary excellence.

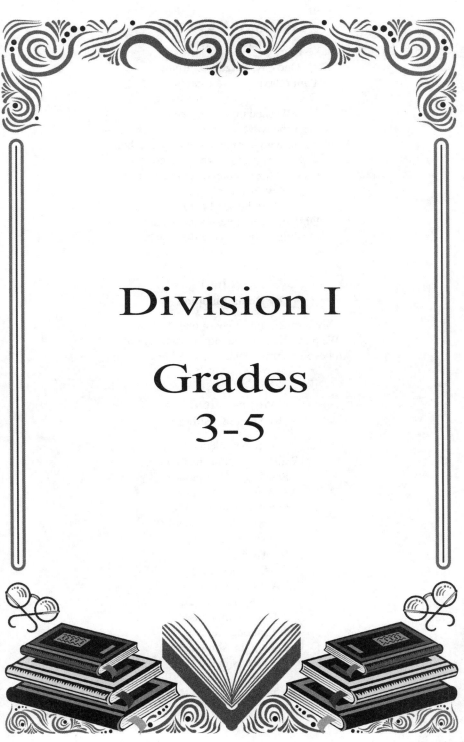

Division I

Grades 3-5

A Day At the Beach
by Victoria Lucarelli

One day, seagulls chirping
I am relaxing on my sandy towel
And a big, gray, ugly shark
Washed up on the sand
I hear the waves, and I see jellyfish
Washing up with bumpy and lumpy seashells
As I am walking up the sand
I see a whole bunch of sand crabs
By my sandy feet
And the sand crabs
Digging deep holes in the ground
And that was a day at the beach.

Kickball
by Raina Shannon

My brother and I love to play kickball.
We play when we get home from school,
And even on the weekends, we play kickball.

Super Silent
by Sheila Cushing

Super silent
Walking most of the time
Sneaking like a puma
Waiting to catch its prey
I wonder why the dog
Visits me from next door?
Always comes
Always comes
Always comes
A little brown dog
Crawls under a gate
Toward my house
That dog, so cute
On a light, shiny day
No clouds in the sky
Super silent

Flowers On Trees
by Thomas McGrath

How long has this tree been here?
Small flowers
Pink like a flamingo
Peaceful
Peaceful
Peaceful
No clouds
Breezy
Birds are singing
From its branches
How old is this tree?
Flowers
Flowers
Flowers
Bright sun shining
All over
The tree.

A Never-Ending Horizon
by Isabelle Souza

How long has this been here?
Peaceful
Blank, like an empty room
With red walls
And a blue and white ceiling
Quiet
Quiet
Quiet
I look, and see
Reds, whites, and browns
All over me
Surrounding my tiny body
As tranquil as a butterfly
A shadowy, hot day
The Grand Canyon
Windy ... quiet ...
A never-ending horizon.

The Dime
by Matthew Wood

A dime on the street
Broken by winds
Polished by rain
New, shiny, and silver
Shining like the moon
Sitting strong and scary
On a walk with my mom and dog.

The Lucky Day
by Ryan Gambo

It was a hot, sunny day in the summer
At the dark blue ocean, walking aside the sand
Suddenly, I see something washed up
It was a hundred dollar bill
I picked it up
The bill was all wet
I kept the washed up, green, soggy
Hundred dollar bill

The Mystery Animal
by Raymond Murphy IV

The Tsankawi desert hill
With the brown plants all over
The holes in the ground
From the mystery animal
And the holes feel like rocks
Have been smoothed and pounded into the ground
But, alas, the mystery animal has not been found

The Old Cat
by Trevor VanBaulen

Inside the old cat, the strong engines will run.
Inside the strong engines, the cat's blood will move.
Inside the cat's blood, the green mountains will grow.
Inside the green mountains, the cat holds the world.
Inside the cat holding the world, the stormy wind grows.
Inside the stormy wind, the oceans will fly.
Inside the flying ocean, the raging mad bull.
Inside the raging mad bull, the old cat.

Look!
by John Carroll

Have birds been here before?
So silent; very peaceful
A tiny breeze:
Whoosh, whoosh, whoosh
A sunny day
Mourning doves flying across the light
As cute as baby
Look!
Then ...
Trees and flower bushes
Other animals, gone in a flash
The doves soar right off the branch!

Lake Ontario
by Megan Barry

So beautiful, that lake
Sun setting, fish swimming
The big orange beating down
Trees so black, sky getting dark
All of the fish starting to go to bed

Green Leaf Tree
by Maeve Leighton

Drip ... drop ... drip ... drop ...
Sun leaving; white clouds
Transforming into gray clouds
Moving in the sky
A beautiful rainbow appears
How does it form?
Watching people
Running under wet
Forest-green trees
Red-orange-yellow-green-blue-purple
Red-orange-yellow-green-blue-purple
Rainbow colors
Fading away
I feel my eyelids fall down.

The Mysterious Sea
by Vincent Guerra

The sea as quiet as ever
His face squeezing for sound about to explode
Hears sounds from miles away
Staring at the clouds about to get pushed up
Finally his sea makes some sound
And he gets pushed up and he hears his sea.

Snow
by Alyssa Anderson

Look out the window!
What's that you see?
It's snow, just like the weather guy said it would be!
How's this for a dream?
I hope you surely want to scream!
White little flurries rolling down to the ground.
They will surely scatter all around!
Inches of snow are piling up now.
Do you know what time it is?
It is now time to play out in the snow!
Overnight it will probably grow.
There will probably be no school tomorrow.
Don't you love snow?

Wrestling
by Noah Pointer

Wrestling
Fake, violent
Announcing the throw and tackle
Exciting, nervous, energized, wondering
That's Wrestlemania!

Spring
by Jamie Atschinow

Dark clouds fill all space
As the gusting wind brushes against my face.
Pitter-patter goes the rain,
For it's falling gently, while the lightning streaks stretch as big as a Great Dane.
I hear a whoosh, then all is still.
The sun comes shining from over a hill.
I dig a hole into the dark soil,
And I drop a few seeds in, as the sun starts to boil.
I cover the hole and sprinkle on some water.
A sprout pops out and becomes a flower.
I hear the birds that love to sing,
As you can tell, this is spring.

Ray Charles
by Matt Sussman

Ray Charles went blind
When he was only seven.
His music continues to play on
Even while he is in Heaven.

Spring
by Autumn Williams

Flowers, chirping, going to the mall
Dancing, singing, running down the hall
Yay! Yay! Spring break's here
Every day, every day, I will cheer
I'll be in California for that week
When I get off the plane, I will speak
"Hurray!"

Ladybugs Soaring
by Natalie Ziemba

Swoosh! Take a look,
A ladybug is passing my garden.
She's red–no, orange!
Wait, I see yellow too!
One thing I know is,
She's spotted, dotted, polka-dotted!
She's in for a peaceful landing,
Flitting, flapping, slower and slower.
Crunch, crunch, crunch,
Now chewing on a purple petal.
Tacky, ticklish, tingling bug,
Now climb up on my arm.
Fly back to your babies,
Float away, I made my wish.

Spiders Can Be Creepy
by Vincent Ruff

Spiders can be very creepy,
Sticky, furry, and fuzzy, too.
Spiders can be scary,
Black, brown, or gray,
Crawling and slithering by.
Many long legs to come sneaking up on you.
Icky, yucky spiders,
Be careful–
They can be poisonous too!

It's Time For Fall
by Chelsea Bell

I love playing outside
You do, too
I love to hear the leaves crunch
You do, too
We all love fall
As much as you do, too

The Pearl Clam
by Chris Fredricks

Once, I saw a clam
It was sad and had no friends
His only friend was his home
I took him home
He opened up
Then he put a little
Dirt in his home
Five years later, in his cage, like a tiny box
There was a pearl next to him
I guess it was the fifth anniversary
For when I found him.

Poor Little Bitty
by Kyla Fellon

There once was a cute little kitty
Her owner named her Bitty
Once, she got wet
Poor little pet
But she still thinks she's so pretty

Bad Day
by Matthew Ryan

Thunder hits the ground
The ground explodes
Then everything jets out
Then the sky turns purple
This all happens because my mom
Said I was moving.

Springtime
by Keshea Brown

I love playing in the sun
I hear the birds chirping
I don't like it when spring is done

Nature All Around
by Awab Hassan

Who am I,
Who am I,
Who am I, you ask?
I am nature,
I'm all around,
Side to side,
You may say.
If you wonder if you are me,
Come and jump to victory!
Try being a tree,
Try being a plant.
If you do that, you are nature, like me!
Go, go, go now,
You are nature to me.
Stretch like a tree to victory!
Hoorah!

Untitled
by Elizabeth Salter

Moving swiftly through the land
Walking with a faded hand
Legs are weak and faded away
Knowing you will always stay
Walking through the world without a care
Knowing no one can see you there
Moving as you please
Talking to the land and trees
Watching upon others down
Never, never wearing a frown
Soft and warm but no embrace
Always seeing a smiling face
Faded, faded, faded away
Always going to stay
Ghost

Little Beetle
by Juwairia Ansari

There was a beetle.
It had a needle.
It poked a prey.
That's the end of the day.
The little beetle went at night
Outside to flight.
He found something that was white.
Then, he took a little bite.
It tasted so bad
That it made him so mad.
He wanted to sleep
Inside a big black jeep.

Flowers
by Krystal Segarra

It's springtime
Flowers are blooming, so bright and beautiful
They make the gardens look so lively
Bumblebees buzzing, flying from flower to flower
They can't stop buzzing because of the pollen
Hummingbirds are flying backwards, getting the nectar from the flowers
Adults, children, and babies sneezing, wheezing
And fighting over who will get the tissues first
I love flowers!

Summer School Is Fun
by Duha AbuEldahab

Summer school is fun!
We get to play and hop.
We get to laugh and gag.
We get to march and harsh.
We get to eat and beat.
We get to munch and punch.
We get to lick and kick.
We get to sleep and peep.
Summer school is fun!
Summer school is done!

A World Crisis
by Austin Bartola

A big beautiful land, you know we love it
But look what we have done to it.
We've cut the trees, we killed the bees
Now we are begging on our knees.
For a better land, to live and play
That's very grand, so, we can say
We have a sky, so big and blue
Alas those dreams may never come true.
The cars and trains, the dirty oil
With all these things, the earth is soiled.
So, stop the pollution, make the sky blue
So all these dreams may all come true!

Seven Angry Faces
by Eddy Avkhukov

Seven crocodiles green
Lots of spikes on their body
Resting in a zoo
Their faces like angry devils
People saying "ooh" and "ahh"
A bright day
But trees covered most of the light
The crocodiles looking at the tourists
And lie down for a long, long, long nap.
Why are they in the giant ditch?

Brother
by Zane Wright

Funny
Talks a lot
Yells too much
Nice to play with
Wears glasses
Good friend to play with
Plays guitar
Kind
Addicted to games

Spring
by Max Freeman

Spring is the time of year
When humans get to peer
At birds singing in the breeze
Through the city, through the trees
If you're up in Marlboro or down in Freehold
Spring is a wonderful thing to behold
Cherry blossoms, pink as cotton candy
Boy, they sure are dandy!
When buds appear on trees
When a person sees
Beautiful, colorful flowers
Followed up by April showers
Exotic, green leaves
Go outside, if you please
Admire this wonderful season
For I have a reason
It's spring, spring, spring
What a wonderful thing!

Who I Am
by Shannon Thaler

When I dance, I feel so free;
It's who I am, it's part of me.
My feet move quickly here and there,
They work together, a perfect pair!
If I couldn't dance, what would I do?
I would sit around, and be bored, too.
The dance floor is my very own stage,
I'm like a bird–just out of my cage.
When I dance, I forget about it all.
Nothing in my head, not even the mall!
My legs stretch wide, my arms have wings.
The air around me starts to sing.
When I dance, I feel so free,
It's who I am, it's part of me.

Springtime
by Alissa Tsai

Gentle winds blow in the sky as the sun shines up high
Everything is delightful to the eye
While the butterflies move around the air, so graceful, like dancers
Are all signs of the cold winter passing while the beautiful spring enters
Putting away the warm and snuggly coats and going out to play
When you can stay in the sun throughout the day
Spring time is like a bird being let out to fly
And you can't resist not letting out a sigh
A tree grows its leaves back
You can take your bicycle off that rusty rack
For it's spring time now, and no more cold weather
You can wear jackets as light as a feather
The flowers' petals open like miracles in the field
A giant tree acts like a shield
Making a home for many animals
The scenery makes happiness in many souls

Yellow
by Alyanna Argueza

Yellow is the color of a topaz gem,
And a buttercup on a slender stem.
Yellow is the color of a happy sun.
It's a lemon, oh, so sour.
Yellow is when you say, "Hi,"
Under the blazing, hot, bright sky.
It is a sign of happiness.
It makes you say, "Yes, yes, yes!"
Sometimes yellow means something bad:
It can mean avarice, and cowardice. Isn't that sad?
Yellow makes you quiver with greed.
It feels like it's everything you need.
Yellow is about hope and summer.
Don't you think yellow is a beautiful color?

White
by Elisa Pancho

White is the snow on a bright winter's day
When cute little polar bears go out to play
White is the clouds on display
Floating about any which way
White is the color of a baby's milk
A bride's wedding gown is white silk
It's the bony antlers on an elk
White is a storm that comes in December
White is the sound of thunder as it goes through the air
White is the cornea of your eye
White is the moon against the black night sky
It's pure, it's innocent, it's cleanliness, and it's fresh
White is the color that is best!

Pumpkins
by Angela Colo

Purple, pink
Pick pink pumpkins
With purple stripes
Said Sally Sue

Beauty In Front of Me
by Montserrat Hernandez

Bright sun
Rustling of leaves
Back and forth
Back and forth
Back and forth
Are there more black-capped chickadees?
So tiny, like little mice
Staring at me with black eyes
Its head bobbing side to side
Sun beams down on us ...
Beauty
Right in front of me

A Great Big View
by Martin Soll

A clear day, with cars moving fast
The air, cool like a breeze
The Hudson River filled with boats ... honking
What building do I see?
The Empire State Building, as tall as the clouds
Down below, streets full of cars
With traffic lights blinking
On the sidewalks, people are walking
Busy city
Busy city
Busy city
New York City
A great big view.

Are They Happy?
by Matthew Fox

A rock waterfall
Splashing water, scattered rocks, grassy floor
A shining sun and a cool shadow
Like paradise
Like paradise
Like paradise
Three foxes with a light
Tapping of paws
Tapping of paws
Tapping of paws
Playful, like me and my friends
Are the foxes happy?
Are they healthy?
These zoo foxes live my paradise ...
My paradise!

Brown Like Chocolate
by Kayla Kolb

Whooshing and whooshing
Your leaves moving
Wind growling like a tiger
A wide trunk, brown like chocolate
Bright sunlight shining on it
Flowers appear
When do they begin growing?
Gives you shade
Animals make it their home
Birds are sometimes silent like the night
Then ... you hear chirping sounds
Birds, birds, birds
How long do you take to grow?

Dreams and Things
by Mia Fondacaro

I have dreams about teams and lean meat.
In my bed, I sleep; when I wake, I eat.
Hear and see the tea whistle and steam.
At night, I watch TV on Channel 33,
With Sam and Melanie,
With a t-shirt on me.
So this is my poem soon-to-be,
So come with me and read it with me,
And you'll see dreams and things.

War and Peace
by Matthew Spooner

Peace
Calm, nice
Loving, caring, sharing
Treaty, harmony, noisy, loud
Fighting, destroying, shooting
Battle, combat
War

Ticklish Ladybugs
by Marissa Rosa

Swoosh, swish, swoosh,
Ticklish ladybugs flying by.
Here, there, up and down,
The ladybugs are everywhere.
Spotted, quiet, peaceful, calm,
Watch the ladybugs pass my yard,
See how ladybugs really are.
Flower to flower, leaf to leaf,
See the ladybugs on all the trees.
Red and black, black and red,
Soaring through the peaceful sky.
Wait, hurry up! Make a wish! Take a minute!
They're lucky fellows, as you can see,
Now, go fly away, and be safe!

Love
by Marlena Malagon

If you're asking if I need you
The answer is forever
If you're asking if I'll leave you
The answer is never
If you're asking what I value
The answer is you
If you're asking if I love you
The answer is I do

Healthy Food
by Kelly Martins

Beans are green,
Carrots are orange,
Apples are red,
Pears are green,
Strawberries are red,
Bananas are yellow,
Mangos are green and red.

Together
by Ian Quinn

Together,
We are a force so strong,
A power so great,
That nothing else could beat us
Together we are united, always,
A country
And will always be together.

Spring
by Katelyn Catana

Spring designs a painted world
Spring announces to the flowers
"It is time to bloom!"
Spring calls the clouds to bring the rain
Birds come, swooping down, to sing winter to sleep

Pieces
by Angela Giampolo

A piece of me is a piece of honesty.
A piece of my dad is a piece of hard work.
A piece of my mom is a piece of truth.
A piece of my sisters is a piece of all personalities.
And all of those pieces make a whole family.

Somewhere
by Allyson Lewis

Somewhere in the world today,
Anything can happen
Lying; believing; trusting others; taking a chance,
Hoping I'll find my dignity,
What could possibly happen
In the world today?
It's different from back then
I'll try whatever it takes;
I'll hope; I'll cry;
Somewhere in the world today,
I'll find the place where I belong.

Earth: My Inspiration
by Kathleen Kelly

We pollute our land, sea, and air.
Not just you and me, but people everywhere.
Turn lights off when you are done,
Or get power from the sun.
If you look around, you may see
Paper products not made from trees.
Cars use gas and gas pollutes!
Use electric cars, and bikes too!
Televisions aren't even fun,
When the amount of people watching is no one.
So turn them off when you leave.
Don't waste electricity, save some trees!
Don't take a car, take a bicycle!
Then we'll all reduce, reuse, and recycle.

Stars
by Samantha Geris

The sky at dusk was long and starry
Just last night the stars secretly guided me
They whispered that if I told I'd be sorry
So to me and the stars the secret will be.
Every night I would give them all a name
Most stars liked them and floated in delight
But when they didn't they would grouch in shame
Either way they all learned to shine big and bright.
And so they took me away
To this far away land
Where I could have fun and play
There would even be a playground surrounded by sand.
Finally, close to morning they took me back
They flew very swiftly as it would seem
The stars threw me on my bed like a sack
I think back now and say, "Sadly, it was only a dream!"

The Beach
by Andrew Post

The beach is salty and sandy
You can't hear the seagulls silently slide down
As they drift through the sunset
You hear the crow of the wonderful birds that wander over the wavy sea
You feel the soft, gentle touch of the super soft sand beneath your feet
When you walk into the aggressive sea, you can feel the rush of the waves
During the night, the gloaming sunset
Will give a reflection off the shimmering waves
When the waves crash on the soft sand
When the sunset reflects off of the sea
You can get a glance of beauty
The sea looks like it never seems to stop

The Nightmare
by Sean Fitzmaurice

I had a nightmare
I was being chased by an insane clown
I sprinted into a dark alley
It was a dead end
I climbed over a huge wall
I terribly hurt my leg
The clown caught me
I had a nightmare

Herman
by Elisabeth Caswell

Loyalty
Faithful, dependable
Relying, devoting, honoring
Always there beside you
Trustworthy

Ninjas
by James Santos

I'm full of anxiousness and fear,
The way of the ninjas is near.
The sound of the swords,
Clang, clang, clang,
And the force of the wood,
Bang, bang, bang.
The way of the ninjas is here,
They can sense their enemies' fear.
The sound of the throwing stars,
Whoosh, whoosh, whoosh,
The sound of the swords slashing,
Swoosh, swoosh, swoosh.
The power of their hands,
While the women practice with fans.
The way of the ninjas is clear,
The way of the ninjas is to force their enemies' fear.

Sea of Life
by Thomas Lampognana

We dived down into the crystal clear sea
Fish swimming around, silence is key
We come around a high mountain of rocks
And see a golden coral city, guarded by sharks
We swim through the city, seeing fishes of all colors
Blue, red, green; little fishes swimming with mothers
A beautiful underwater forest of green
A wonderful place no one has ever seen
We swam through the jungle with gentle care
Trying not to disturb the creatures that lived there
And, in the center, where all the fishes swam
Laid an enormous clam
And in the clam laid a giant pearl
That shone like the stars and had a Milky Way swirl
A faint, small beep: my air is low
And to the surface I must go
The beeping was my alarm clock it seems
Then I jerk up from my midnight dreams
But, maybe, that pearl with the sparkle and shine
Someday, oh, someday, the pearl might be mine

Aurora Borealis
by Niki Maragos

Sitting silently by the bay
Watching the day calmly fade away
The sky sweetly turns to a yellowish gray
Transforming now to a crimson red
The enthusiasm never dead
To behold the essence of night
Just to watch the silent light

Spring Fun
by Alyson Brockmann

Flowers are blooming,
Children are playing.
Airplanes are zooming,
And some people are saying
That spring awaits
And we can't wait,
For April showers
To bring May flowers.

Alone
by Timothy Ruszala

A tulip in a flock of daisies.
It stands out.
It knows it is not the same,
But still, it yearns to be welcomed.
Other flowers are born,
They look identical to their parents.
The tulip wonders,
"Why wasn't I born normal?
Why do I have to be so different?"
The tulip did not get an answer, nor did it ever.
The tulip was miserable,
No friends, no fun, just hatred,
But the tulip knew one thing for sure.
The one who stands out is the first to be seen.
The first who is seen, is the first to be picked.
The first to be picked, is the first to be admired.
The tulip dreamt, and dreamt, until the day his dream came true.

Basketball's My Favorite Sport
by Joey Sauchelli

Basketball's my favorite sport.
I dribble up and down the court.
The ball goes bouncing off my toes
And beans the teacher in the nose.
He stumbles back and grabs his nose
And hits the wall, and down he goes.
The other players stop and stare,
They've never heard the teacher swear.
With no one playing anymore
I grab the ball. I shoot. I score.
I love this game! It's so much fun.
The teacher cried, but, hey–we won!

Friends
by Dominique Martino

I like you, you like me
We're both friends, we both agree
I call you, you call me
We always play, every day
Me and you, you and me
We'll be friends
Until the end of history

Mom
by Lydia Whitaker

When thunder is near
And you're full of fear
You know where to run
Go to the one who's always fun
Your mom!

The Garden
by Paris Doherty

In the garden, silent and sweet,
Roam small little creatures, oh, so neat.
They crawl and they wiggle,
They shake and they giggle,
Until the day grows cold,
And the night grows old.
First thing in the next day,
They sing and they play.
"Have a great day!" they say
As they sway with the wind.
As the day grows cold and the nights grow old,
They settle to sweet dreams of the next day,
Which will have them all shouting, "Hurray!"

The Cure
by Heather Robinson

There was an old lady
Had to tie her shoe
She had nothing but the flu
There was no cure
Except a pedicure
Which only gave her shiny toes

The Kite
by Thomas Tauche

High, yellow
Laughing, fun, cheerful
Windy, sky, string, diamond
Fancy ribbon, plastic
Cool

Pizza
by Gavin Homan

Cheesy, cheesy, cheesy
Delicious, delicious, tasty
Tasty, delicious, delicious
Tasty, tasty, hot
Hot, hot, tasty
Tasty, tasty, hot
Hot pizza
Very, very
Tasty; very
Very hot
I love
Pizza
Very
Much.

Scooter
by Terrahja Young

I have a dog.
His name is Scooter.
He is black and he has big brown eyes.
He has floppy ears.
He likes to play and run.
His favorite sport is soccer.

Sunsets
by Jaina Shannon

Sunset is like a beautiful thing
It can happen anywhere
It is just like a rainbow
But it does not happen after the rain.
Sunsets make me believe in myself
I have confidence in myself every time I see one!
Sunsets are as if you are on a beach
Sitting on your beach towel
In front of a hot sunset.

Moods
by Demoan Giunta

I have moods that you have
You have moods that I have
When I'm sad, I start to cry
When I'm happy, I laugh and play
Some moods are different
When I'm angry, I yell and scream
These are the moods I can be in
But there are more I cannot explain
Those moods feel funny inside
Most moods, to me, are good ones
Those are the ones I'm normally in

Chocolate
by Katherine Reilly

Chocolate is good to eat,
And is very sweet!
Chocolate is usually wrapped in tin foil.
Just like filling a car with gas,
You have to eat chocolate, or you will not last!
There is dark chocolate and milk chocolate,
No matter what kind of chocolate,
Chocolate is always good.
Not to like chocolate, you've got to be in a very bad mood.

Cherry Blossom Trees
by Cassandra Yap

Cherry blossom trees,
They grow pink, beautiful leaves.
What happiness they bring,
Because they grow in the spring.
I wouldn't be happy at all,
Because they grow in the fall.
People take pictures of them in Japan,
So I'll probably see them my whole life span.

My Dad's Boat
by Lucas Mazzarella

My dad's boat is not that big, but it's big enough.
My dad's boat is strong enough to hit large waves.
My dad's boat is fast enough to win in a race.
My dad's boat is nice enough to win a contest.
My dad's boat is likely enough to carry five big fish.

Spring
by Kaycie Elifani

Time to play with friends
Baby animals are born
Rain showers are here

Birds
by Kelsey Peterson

The birds chirp at dawn
And sing a beautiful song
To let the wonderful day begin
With unique words
And end a great day
With a relaxing song
To soothe your soul

Am I
by Olivia Ray

I pounce as I whiz by
Fast and fearless, a cheetah am I.
I sing as I soar through the bright blue sky
Quick and nimble, a bluebird am I.
I cry to the moon way up high
With my sad echoing howls, a gray wolf am I.
I'm here, then I'm gone in the blink of an eye
Scared and shy, a chameleon am I.
I made my home, then along came a fly
He got stuck in my web, a spider am I.
I get into bed and I sigh a great sigh
Out of this world, a dreamer am I.

I Am
by Genedi Muniz

I am outgoing, and strong
I wonder if the world will ever change
I hear someone calling from Heaven
I see shadows dancing
I want to go to college
I am outgoing, and strong
I pretend to share my real emotions with others
I feel an angel patting my back saying, "It's okay."
I touch a wolf's soft fur
I worry that my family might get sick
I cry when my family is in pain
I am outgoing, and strong
I understand why my parents do certain things for me
I say that all human beings should be tolerant
I dream that the world will be successful
I try to do better in school
I hope for a miracle
I am outgoing, and strong

Anxiety
by Anna Henderson

As the tension builds up,
My pupils widening,
My soul falling,
I can almost feel the tears.
Stomach starts turning,
Good thoughts pop,
Just like a balloon.
Those voices telling me,
"Nothing will be OK."
I can feel the tears.
I wish they were gone.
As the sweat drips down my face,
Plop, plop, plop,
Drop by drop, sweat falls.
I can barely stand.
I can finally see the tears just running down
My face like a waterfall
But I know it will be OK.

Summary
by Steven Oliveros

Summer is hot
Summer is cool
In summer we do lots of things
We eat ice cream
We play with friends
We also go on vacation, we mostly go to the beach
We get wet by the waves
We play with and in the sand
Then we get to go to the library and do homework
We go to the arena to watch sports and entertainment
We visit relatives
We eat fish in the summer
Summer, summer, summer, summer

Earth Day
by Shivani Majmudar

Today the Earth has changed.
The trees are cut down,
The birds make no sound,
Today the Earth has changed.
The animals walk the barren land,
As their eyes question each man,
They think we banded together to harm,
Instead we lend a helping hand.
We plant a seed or two,
Get rid of all the weed,
Plant a berry bush for their need,
And realize we did a good deed.
Now our Earth is a rich, lush world,
It's like a blue-green pearl,
That stands out from the rest,
Amongst all the dirt.
This is why we celebrate Earth Day,
You should care and help us in any way
We want to be the blue-green pearl,
That won't be brushed away.

Cars
by Angel Cordero

Don't ask what's under my hood
Try finding out if you could
The turbo makes the engine faster
Don't turn it into a disaster!
My Volkswagen is the best
It's going to be in Waterfest
It's going to be so hot
I'll give it every part I got

Outside
by Jennifer Kurzweil

The sun is shining outside
The bluebirds are flying high in the sky.
A girl is jumping very high
She scraped her knee and said goodbye.
Tomorrow's another day that she can try
To try her luck at catching a fly.
Maybe one day, she could fly high in the sky.
She wished and wished, and it came true, so she jumped up
And then she started to fly way up high.
She was very happy that she could fly
With the birds in the sky.
A small girl that made her dream come true
Just by wishing, so why don't you?

Funky Monkeys
by Killeen Williams

Monkeys are funky in all different ways
They can swing, jump, and play all day
They can swing from tree to tree
But, yet, can't tell knee from knee
They eat bananas while swinging on a vine
While leaping crazily in one straight line
They bob up and down, doing funky dances
Performing all different prances
Funky monkeys are awesome!

My Cat Cleo
by Dana Schioppo

I have a cat that chases mice,
Around the house she is nice.
Although she is an older cat, she plays and runs around.
Sometimes she hides without a sound
And pounces as you walk around.
Although she weighs eleven pounds,
She can always play an extra round.
My cat is named Cleo and she is the best,
Far better than all the rest.

My Curious Cat
by Mary Nowak

My cat scurries like a rat
And jumps like a spring
And crashes with a bash.
He chases the mouse
Around the house,
And then runs outside as he
Climbs up the tree to chase a bee
Then he comes back to the house
And runs to me.

Skiing
by Madalyn Zuber

Skiing is so much fun.
The excitement that fills me is great.
I love seeing all the happy people and snow.
When I look at the mountain, a huge smile spreads across my face.
Every trail is different.
They are rated green, blue, black, and double black.
Skiing is such a fun sport.
Maybe one day, you'll try it too.

Baseball
by Nickolas Androvett

Baseball is America's game.
There are many famous names.
The crowd is chanting.
While the breeze is panting.
When you win you're glad.
But when you lose you're sad.
Baseball is just a game.
But people will never forget your name.
A baseball is white.
But it is very bright at night.
Like Mickey Mantle.
To newcomers like Rick Fantle.
Baseball is a game of fun.
Even if you have one mile to run.

Time Machine
by Kyle Parker

I checked out the Civil War
I thought it would be a bore
The guns went rat-tat-tat
Lincoln gave me his hat
The Chicago Fire was so sad
Edison made everyone glad
Borrowed the light bulb, forgot to return it
Tom laughed, and then told me I'd earned it
I saw the young King Tutankhamun
He had an odd house that's not very common
He gave me the head of a crocodile
He killed it one day, at the bay of the Nile
Einstein was cool; gave me a test tube
I taught him to make some good food
Yes, all of those people were kind
I then left in my time machine I built in my mind

It's Easier
by Nicolás Sarmiento Arias

It is easier to wait an eternity,
Than not looking for where you are
It's easier to make all the honey bitter of a honeycomb,
Than not singing for you
It's easier to count the sand of the sea,
Than not fall in love with you
It is easier to catch a shooting star,
Than not to write poems for you
It is easier to breathe under water,
Than not wish for you to be near me
It is easier to inhabit the solar system,
Than not believe in you
It is easier to find a needle in a haystack,
Than not pray for you
Everything is easier, sweeten the water, let it embrace
I do not want, nor can I leave to love, I live only for love,
For you're carried in my mind and in my heart,
Second by second, minute by minute, and hour by hour.

It's Not Cool
by Melisa Onc

Heads up! Straight down!
I need to know if you're coming around,
I need to know if you're here
To see if you're not drinking beer.
'Cause, if you are
You can't steer the car
'Cause if you are, you are weird
How could you? It's bad for you,
It's not cool! Drinking beer is lame.
'Cause if you are, it's a stupid decision.
I hope you are not drinking beer
Even though some people think it's dumb
It's actually a smart decision
And I'm so happy you're not drinking beer!

Leafy Trees
by Kristina Fields

Leafy trees, leaves all around us,
On the twigs and branches,
Where the snow used to fall
Down from the cloud
To the hills below.
Now all the robins sing,
In the twilight, twilight,
Making beautiful songs.
Little leaves blow in the air,
Making wonderful noise
Up on the hills, and down in the valleys
Everywhere, everywhere.

My Secret Garden
by Natalie Laliberte

Hidden deeply in the woods
My treasure is hard to find
Once abundant, now endangered, because of mankind
Peeking through its compost blanket
Beneath the beech, birch, and maple trees
Drops of rain and rays of sunlight help my garden grow
Picked away by modern day, they're scarcely alive
I'll always grow my ginseng and golden seal garden
To help them, and us, survive

Summertime
by Rachel McCann

The blazing hot sun beats down on me.
So I drink cool, delicious lemonade to cool down ...
Seeing kids make sandcastles,
While I tan on my blue, dotted towel.
School is out too!
So you can relax, because all your worries
Are down the drain.

A Is For Apple
by Alexa Mullins

A, B, C
1, 2, 3
One is for you, and one is for me
Sit in a circle–wait your turn
Snack time and recess
Stickers to earn
So much to learn
So much to see
Kindergarten teacher
That's for me

Fifth Grade
by Eddie Lesko

Fifth grade, fifth grade
Time flies by
It is almost time to say the antonym of hi
Sixth grade seems scary
Like a monster who is hairy
I will not decline
And I will not whine
I will not start raid,
By the way, I'm only in first grade!

Everything Is Growing
by Gloriana Alvarado

Grounds are wet
Trees are slippery
Ponds are filled
As little drops
Fall into it
The bids chirp
The squirrels climb
Everything is growing

I Love God's Creations
by Monica Bakare

I love the sun, I love the moon, I love the stars up in the sky.
I love my mom, I love my dad, I love the flowers in the ground.
I love my sisters, I love the leaves that fall off the great big tree.
I love the animals I see at the zoo; parrots, bears, and other things too.
I love the fishes in the water, swimming in different directions and ways.
I love the clouds. They are fluffy and white. They're nice to look at up in the sky.
I love the raindrops beating on my window; pitter-patter is the sound it makes.
I love the birds that chirp and chirp, singing songs all day long.
I love the whole wide world, because God made it for you and me!

No Pollution
by Rodney Byun

Nature is around me
The sun is in the sky
The leaves are in the trees
The flowers come from Earth
The fish are in the sea
Our mother is in danger
Our mother, Mother Earth
Reduce, reuse, recycle
Celebrate her birth

Summer
by Jayson Green

Summer is almost here.
So, everyone, give a cheer!
The plants and trees will grow so high.
They will almost reach the aquamarine sky.
Children will run and play.
They will stay out all day.
The summer sun will begin to set again soon
And the days will end with a gleaming moon.
That's when the leaves will change, and turn maroon
But until that time arrives
Enjoy the sparkling blue sky.
Summer is almost here.
So, everyone, give a cheer!

Winter Eyes
by Michael Berwanger

Look at winter
With winter eyes
Look up at the
White and gray skies.
Breathe in winter
Past winter nose
Smell the evergreens
Scent of the pine cones.
Walk through winter
With winter feet
For your warmth
Inside warms your feet of sleet.
Listen to winter
With winter ears
You can hear
The sound of the prancing deer.

I Am
by Magdalena Baranowska

I am a girl lost in a world with people at war.
I wonder if there will be peace in the world?
I hear the cry of the people constantly at war.
I see horrible things happening in my imagination.
I want no war for centuries!
I am a girl lost in the world with people at war.
I pretend I'm a soldier fighting for the sake of my country.
I feel anger rush through my body when war comes up.
I touch my grandfather as if he was going to fight.
I worry that war will never end.
I cry when another person is killed in this gruesome war.
I am a girl lost in a world with people at war.
I understand that people hate war.
I say I demand peace.
I dream of flowers blooming and no gunshots in the world.
I try to forget war, but it always comes back.
I hope that there will be peace in the world.

A Wolf's Day
by Luke Hoffman

I am a little wolf
Grrr, grrr, grrr
I can jump up in the air
That's how I catch my fair share
Grr, grr, grr
Next, I tear it into shreds
From toe to head.
Now I have my share of fun
Now it's time to howl at the moon
Now that the day is done.

My Weekend
by Emily Taddei

Today, in school, our teacher asked our class
What we did yesterday, over the weekend.
She called on me, and I told her that I went fishing and caught a bass.
She said, "Wow," and, "That's great! How big was it?"
I didn't quite hear her, so I just went on with my story.
"Since dead fish don't do anything ... well, that's what it did: nothing
But, we did something last night: we ate."
"Outstanding," she said, "But, how big was it?"
I said "Twenty feet long."
Then the whole class was happy for me
So they all stood up and sang me my favorite song.
So I said to the class, "So, that's pretty much all that I did yesterday
So, if you liked it, go ahead and shout hooray!
Though, if you didn't like my story, and you thought it was a bore,
Or if you wanted to sleep, and start to snore,
Also, if you wanted to fall asleep and drool
Then, let me just tell you something, fool.
At least you didn't have to sit up at that stool
Or tell this story to people who are dumb,
That are just sitting there and sucking their thumbs.
So, if you still feel a need to say boo,
Remember what I told you when I'm hitting you with my shoe.
And, class, there is just one more thing that I would like to say
And those two words are thank you!"

I Am
by Danny Rocha

I am a flower in a field
I am a bird in the forest
I am a bug in the desert
I am a shrimp in the ocean
I am a day in a century
I am one out of a million
I am nobody...

Baseball
by Trey Meaux

Spring is baseball time
It's my time to shine
Baseball all the time

My Pencil Can Speak German
by Taylor Gautier

My pencil can speak German
My pencil can speak French
My pencil can say "Hi!"
Or "Quick! Behind that bench!"
My pencil can speak Japanese
And he'll speak Chinese, too
My pencil can say "Howdy!"
And "Hey! How do you do?"
There's one problem with my pencil
It's something I should mention
My pencil badmouthed teachers
And now I'm in detention

The Wind
by Nicholas Ferrer

The wind whispers to me like a lonely child
It signs a low and quiet song
It asks to come in
I listen to it fondly in my bedroom
Till its low, quiet song puts me fast asleep

School
by Haley Croteau

School is an awesome thing to do during the days
Monday, Tuesday, Wednesday, Thursday, and Friday
With lots of nice teachers and kids
School is when the teachers tell you a lot of things
So, everyday you learn, and learn, and learn
So you can be smart for college, and graduate

Nature
by Jessica Lasky

When May flowers come,
April showers go
In May the sun gets brighter
And the grass gets greener
And the water gets cooler
May is a happy month.

Lego
by Brian Bido

Fantasy with building–click!
A piece has fallen–pop!
Oh, no! The ship has crashed–crash!
Let's build again–click, clack, clack!

Living In a Never Ending Nightmare
by Melissa Baker

The cure to this disease is what I crave
Before my name appears on a grave
Tears met my eyes while trying to contain
The horrible thing that's causing me pain
A life of endless fighting, day and night
If the cure is found, I'll see the light
Struggling and suffering all the way
With radiotherapy every day
At night, I cry myself to sleep
No one hears my silent weep
Thank you, Susan G. Komen, for helping me
Destroy breast cancer happily.

La Charca
by Aileen Mayorga

Cuando el viento esta fuerte el pino se mueve y dice "aiiiiaii"
Los sapos saltan y se meten al lodo y también dicen "aiiiiaii"
El zorro ve las nubes blancas como algodón.
Y corre de tras de las nubes de algodón.
Nunca alcanza las nubes y dice "aiiiiaii"
Todos saben que viene el otoño y dicen "aiiiiaii"

Dolly's Hat
by Sarah Snook

Dolly had a mat,
Dolly had a cat,
But Dolly's most prized possession was her hat
She wore it into town,
She never dropped it on the ground
She even chose it over a crown
Her hat was white, with purple polka-dots
They were polka-dots, but she called them spots
Even though she had a mat and a cat
Dolly's most prized possession was her hat

My Oasis
by Natalie van Oyen

The waves splash
The seagulls sing
I look into the sun
It glares in my eyes
I hear the ocean's voice
Calling out to me
I wonder why?
I step forward into the sand
Then the earth is still
The only thing that seems alive
Is the ocean as deep as blue
I hear it whistling in my ear
Oh, the wonders it makes when
I'm near
At the deep blue ocean
More likely known as "The Beach"

Talking To the Wind
by Amber Sullivan-Santiago

The wind blowing on the street
That had the colors of all the colors of the rainbow
Shaped like swirls of a cinnamon bun
But not to be seen
Blowing to and fro, pushing trees and bushes
As I hear the shifting sounds
Of the blowing winds
Until, one day,
I came upon a sound in the wind
The wind talking, talking to me, saying
"You are a brilliant, child,
Very talented
But no one can be perfect."
That's what the wind said

The Morning Starts the Day
by Serenity Metz

Oh, how the morning starts my day,
I love the way the air smells!
I love the way the fog is creamy and thick
You probably can't see a stick
Morning, you're quick and still
Nothing moving, not even a windmill
Nature and climate peaceful and calm
Not hot enough to sweat in each palm
Air so very moist
Air so moist, isn't able to hoist
Lovely, pretty flowers
Some with pretty powers
Animals love to run
That means time for fun!
Nice, big tree
Hope it won't sting a bee
Oh, please
I love morning and it loves me!
A lovely way
The morning to start my day!

I'll Come Back
by Al-Nafi Walker

I will come back to hug you.
I will come back to kiss you.
I will come back to watch over you.
I will come back forever and ever.
I will come back.

My State New Hampshire
by Katie Pelletier

It has flowers and rain showers, my state New Hampshire
It has flowers and rain showers, autumn leaves on trees,
My state New Hampshire
It has flowers and rain showers, autumn leaves on trees,
Birds of all kinds that you can never imagine in your mind,
My state New Hampshire
It has flowers and rain showers, autumn leaves on trees
Birds of all kinds that you can never imagine in your mind,
Fishing and swimming, my state New Hampshire
It has flowers and rain showers, autumn leaves on trees,
Birds of all kinds that you can never imagine in your mind,
Fishing and swimming, there are animals here and there,
Everywhere, my state New Hampshire
It has flowers and rain showers, autumn leaves on trees,
Birds of all kind that you can never imagine in your mind,
Fishing and swimming, my state New Hampshire
It has flowers and rain showers, autumn leaves on trees,
Birds of all kinds that you can never imagine in you mind,
My state New Hampshire
It has flowers and rain showers, autumn leaves on trees,
My state New Hampshire
It has flowers and rain showers, my state New Hampshire
It's our state New Hampshire,
It's our state New Hampshire

Untitled
by Jennifer McGrogan

Pass it
Kick it down the field
Dribble, shoot
As they make a shield
I fell to the ground
The crowd is hushed
They take a knee
As I gather my dignity
I walk off the field
With my head held high
They clapped and cheered
As I walked on by

Ice Cream
by Breana Celebrano

Ice cream, ice cream is a good treat.
Some flavors are really sweet.
Everyone likes to eat ice cream.
I even think about it in my dreams.
If it were up to me, I would eat it every day.
I would even eat it by the bay.
Strawberry, chocolate, and pistachio too,
I would even eat it if it were pale blue.
I love ice cream, and I always will.
But my dad might pass out when he sees the bill!

Evil
by Kunaal Chaudhari

Evil is pitch black, dark
It is crushing, screaming, bloody, fatal
None can resist evil
Evil is ugly, heartbreaking, stealing, lying
Evil is powerful, unstoppable
Unless ...
Good is fighting it!

Math Test
by Haris Zia

I'm in school, finishing my math test,
It's really quiet, but soon I hear noises
Tick, tock, tick, tock, goes the clock,
I hear people knocking on their desks
And the door screeching
I hear people slamming lockers
With a great big thud!
The teacher opens his mouth, and says
"Ding, ding, ding," like an alarm clock,
And I found out I was only dreaming.

Spring
by Amanda Bilas

Pink, and red, and yellow, and green,
Buds are always being seen,
Trees are colorful and bright,
What a beautiful sight!
Soon to be a catastrophe,
For those who have an allergy.

Exercise
by Kyra Robinson

I can hear the cars honking
I can hear the people walking
As their feet hit the hot concrete
Fire fighters rushing through the city
Trying to save another life
Can you realize?
If you bully the people you love
They're going to get their revenge
Our future is more important than our past
Can you believe it?
We need to see the world is important
Why do you ask? Because we are important: you and me
I can hear the cars honking
I can hear the people walking
As their feet hit the hot concrete
Invest in your future
The youth are your future
Success is in our reach

Daydreams
by Deborah Besser

You can go to wonderful places.
Places only you can go.
Places no astronaut or explorer can go
Because only you can even imagine
That amazing, interesting, far away land
Of your magnificent, immeasurable daydreams.

My Wish
by Kevin Vass

I wish! I wish!
I get to play
Basketball for Duke
And make it to the National Basketball Association
To play for an amazing
Team!

First Day of School Morning
by Sarah Eldib

When I woke up in the morning, on the first day of school
I would always wonder if I am going to be cool
My mom would always try to drag me out of bed
But instead, I would play dead
"Wake up! Wake up!" my Mom would shout
Of course, I would try to push her out
But, when I go to the bathroom, I would always be mad
Because my lil' sissy would call me bad
I can't say anything to my lil' sissy
Because my mom would always give her kissies
I wish I had a good first day of school morning
But what could you say? I have a feeling that it will never be adoring
When I walk down the stairs
I would sit in my chair
Waiting for a breakfast meal
But what's left in my plate is just a banana peel
I hate the first day of school morning
Again, because it is never adoring
And, next year, it will start again.

Spring Has Sprung
by Janine Skedzielewski

Pop! Pop! Pop!
I can see the tulip's top
The daffodils are coming up
It's time to put them in a cup
Plenty of green grass under my feet
The sound of birds going tweet, tweet, tweet
Spring comes in like a lion and goes out like a lamb
I'm happy it's spring, I am, I am!

Fish Tales
by Michael Spadavecchia

We were on a rented boat, resting afloat.
I wish I could catch a fish.
We hooked our lines with bait, then I had to wait.
But the heat from the sun dried my throat.
As I set down my pole, wouldn't you know,
There was a tug from down below.
The water was dark, then up popped a shark!
Its teeth were white as snow.
My dad picked it up. It was a pup.
He threw it back to the bay.
It was gray. It knew its way.
To be caught another day.

Races
by Swetha Ramesh

Races, spaces, I love races!
Feel the wind in your faces
Your socks so sweaty from the run
Speed is so special, nothing can beat it
First doesn't matter; second doesn't either
Just have fun; it's what you're there for!
Just enjoy it; love it!
Races, spaces, I love races!

April Showers
by Melanie Cooper

April showers bring beautiful flowers
That glisten in the sunlight and makes a lawn bright.
April showers grow trees and trees give a great, great breeze.
April showers leave behind rainbows that glow.
April showers help grass grow and help oxygen flow.

Nightmare
by Minh Vu

Going to sleep.
Has a frightening nightmare.
Walks around the empty field.
Curious; walks in an abandoned house
Ghost chases; sprints
Alarm clock rings.
Wakes up, goes to school
Homework
Bored; watches television
Spots a scary movie; scared
Going to sleep.

Breast Cancer Has No Shine
by Madeline Maguire

Suffering in bed all the time
In a world with no shine.
In a life with not one friend
Breast cancer seems to make your life end.
I heard her weeping; I didn't cry
And now she's gone without a bye.
When I walked through that door
I wanted a breast cancer cure.
When I held her hand for the last time
I hoped her life had a little shine.

Harry Potter
by Farwa Shakeel

It's full of action and adventure,
With ghouls, ghosts, and monsters,
Talking pictures, and flying brooms.
You know it better as Harry Potter.
It's full of magical creatures
And chambers full of secrets,
With tournaments for three.
You know it better as Harry Potter.
It's full of werewolves, and animaguses,
And men with two faces.
You know it better as Harry Potter.
It's full of dark demons and death eaters,
And one mass murderer.
You know it better as Harry Potter.
It's full of Voldemort on his tail,
Blood, battle, and war.
You know it better as Harry Potter.
He always wins these wars
With confidence, love, and friendship,
That's what it's all about.
It's Harry Potter.

I Am a Baseball
by Patrick McAteer

White as snow, cardinal stitched, and circular.
I twist and turn in midair while the cold breeze blows by.
The hard wood crashes against my body.
I thump from the bat's strike.
I look down to see
The players jetting by.
I soar through the air.
Frightened and scared
Twisting and turning
Hovering high
Praying to be caught in the soft leather glove
Before my fall to the ground.

Goodbye Winter, Hello Spring
by Elizabeth Philbrook

Goodbye winter chills, hello warmth
Goodbye Christmas, hello Easter
Goodbye heavy jackets, hello rain coats
Goodbye bald trees, hello spring buds
Goodbye turkey, hello popsicles
Goodbye sledding, hello biking
Goodbye indoor games, hello outdoor games
Goodbye sniffles, hello fresh air

Spring and Summer
by Veronica Wieczorek

Spring and summer are the best of all seasons
They make your heart filled with a sweet and warm feeling
And are the best seasons of them all
You will truly love spring and summer
But not as much as I do

Time Waits For No One
by Moorea Cioppa

"Tick tock" says the clock.
Sigh.
'Cause everybody knows that time is slipping by.
Everybody wishes they had more time,
'Cause then they could do things at the drop of a dime.
But no, clocks can't go backwards because then that would be a hazard.
For the people who wish to turn time back
Because then they could be having a Sunday dinner of fish.
But no, clocks can't go backwards.
So put this in your mind,
Your living and learning is based on a time line, which isn't over ...
Yet.

The Spring
by Dominic Cotugno

Roses are red, violets are blue
Spring is here, so are you.
The trees and flowers bloom, and so do you.
All the animals come out of their dens and welcome spring.
The wide open plain of flowers looks like the spring.
It will not ever, ever end
So come along and enjoy the spring.

Growing Clouds
by Rohan Mallya

Little puffs of white clouds
Always growing bigger and bigger
Always growing grayer and grayer
Until, one day
Thou shall rain
Till all is gone,
But you shall see
More puffs of white clouds
Growing bigger and bigger.

My Parents
by Nikki Kurian

I love my parents.
In the saddest times to the times I love,
They're always there, no matter what.
They help me all the time.
When I do anything, they support me 110%.
My whole life is because of them,
And I will never forget that.
When anything goes wrong, they're always there to help.
They never let me down.
When I do anything and fail, they're there for me, too.

Stars In the Night
by Morgan VanDoren

I watch the stars in the night,
They always shine so bright.
Glooming so high in the sky,
The birds stare while they fly.
The stars playing, they fly so high,
They are just saying hi when they pass by.
Stars in the night are so yellow,
Swaying around, they are so mellow.

Nature
by Max Nelson

Nature is a beautiful sight.
Stars twinkle within the black night.
From distance, nature looks so mellow.
And the sun burns a bright yellow.
The oceans glisten a light blue,
And cows give a great moo.
Yes, nature is a fantastic sight.
Nature makes you feel so bright.

Death
by Matthew Miller

As I stand alone in silence
Against the pale yellow grass
While I stare at the
Charcoal black coffin
Knowing its miserable contents
The spirits drift around me
And when I try to run
I end where I've begun
In an endless fog

The Moment
by Ashley Glen

Anxiously standing there,
Waiting for the moment.
People clapping.
Heart pounding.
The curtain opens.
Music sings a slow introduction.
Gracefully, bodies move across the stage.
I am a leaf, slowly falling down to the ground.
The music gets faster and I am picked up in a windstorm.
Slow again, I land on the ground.
Lights go down.
Music stops.
Final pose.
People clapping.
Heart pounding.

Lizard Life
by Anya Swinchoski

Pounce. Jump. Look!
A cricket. Grab the biggest, juiciest cricket!
Ha, ha! I got more food than you!
Slurp down that worm with delight.
Chew. Swallow.
Get more food. Yum.
Resting time.
Hide where my owner can't find me. Ha, ha!
Skin turns white. Time to shed. Chomp my skin!
Rip it off. Eat it. Spit it. Creep my owner out!
I'll go to my hiding place again.
Goodnight.

Sweet Spring Song
by Shannon Foley

Laughing, colorful flowers bloom joyfully.
The fresh scent of dew surfs through the air.
The sun smiles down on spreading happiness.
Rain sprinkles from floating clouds.
As butterflies swim along with the current of the whispering wind.

Three Languages and Two Worlds
by Ana Subashi

I had two languages that I know,
And one world,
But then I came here which adds
More things in my life,
I never know how to speak this language,
And it took three months to speak it,
I went to ESL, and it helped me very much,
But now in 4th grade I use everything I know,
And it helps
Now I know three languages,
And two worlds.

Basketball Fun!
by Peter Sourbis

Basketball, basketball, basketball
Fun, fun, fun
I hate when the season is done
I love the sport so much
That I play everyday
Dribble, dribble, dribble
Run, run, run
Look out, here I come!
Steal, steal, steal
Score, score, score
We won by four!

Spring Has Sprung
by Dalton Aversa

Spring has sprung,
It's so beautiful.
The Phillies are getting ready for opening day.
I love the smell of the rosy red flowers.
At night, I like to look up at the black, sacred sky,
Sprinkled with gold stars.
I like to play with my awesome friends.
Spring has sprung!

What Matters Most
by Julia Novick

I do not know what's beyond the grave.
That's why I'm scared,
But it doesn't seem brave.
Is life beyond, life at all?
Or is it just,
An endless hall?
It's hard to accept it.
That I'll really be gone,
But I know that forever,
My spirit lives on.
And in the end,
When it's your turn,
You're time to go,
Remember this:
What matters eternally,
What matters most,
Is that loved ones live on
And you're memory,
Is always more, than just a ghost

Spring
by Emma Corazza

Spring, spring, it's time for spring
So many things happen in the spring
Sometimes you see butterflies
Flying in the skies
You can see a lot of bunnies
Sometimes they look really funny
You will see a lot of flowers
There will also be spring showers
There will be some light from the sun
While you play, and have fun, fun, fun

Summer Nights
by Elly Raisch

Gentle breeze, night air
Soft grass, nice and fair
Moon rises in the sky
As the sun says goodbye
Walking gently, steady pace
No running, not a race
Reaching home, such a delight
As I lie down for the night

Biological Weather
by Simon Yang

As the sun sets on your life,
You recall the ever-changing moments of the experience
From blistering 100 degree days and blazing desert travels
To pouring thunderstorms and soccer ball sized hail,
There's always a beautiful sunset worth remembering
And, after you're done flashbacking through your time on this planet,
You discover that it's no fun with weather forecasts

Everything About Me
by Nathalia Chas

The moon shined with its beautiful colorful light at my mother when I was born
My path my mom gave me with my creative mind with my colorful creations
After Pre-K, the kindergarten teacher
Made the light in my future brighter than ever.
When my grandparents died,
The beautiful clouds in my mind turned darker than space.
Now, I have very nice teachers in 5th grade who support everyone to do better
So my knowledge gets bigger and bigger with them.

Poetry
by Yusra Siddiqui

When I try to make poetry
All the pressure is put on me
I know this is a contest
But it feels like a huge test
At first, I didn't know what to write
Because nothing seemed right
Then this topic caught my eye
But, you might ask, why?
Because this is true
It might happen to you
Everyone needs time to make poetry
Everyone! You and me
No one can make a poem really fast
If they do, it might win last
Some people need time
To make a rhyme
Think before you write
Because, sometimes, it might not sound right
You never know what you can find in poetry
To write, one must imagine and believe

Winter Eyes
by Andrew Bruno

Look at winter
With winter eyes
See the snowflakes twirling
As they fall before your very eyes.
Breath in winter
Past winter nose
Pine nettles flow in the air
As the smell flows through your nose.
Walk through winter
With winter feet
Try to stay up
But you just fall back down with ice crackling.
Listen to winter
With winter ears
Noises flow
Through your ears, as you hear the branches crack.

Lisa Myles
by Scott J. Dudas

A family of four,
She was living fine
Two lungs, and one started to fade.
Two boys that she thought she would never have,
No one thought she'd be gone at forty-five.
Fingerprints of blood on the counter
Summer's day when we got a call.
Now a family of three
My eyes started to water.
Stains of blood in her hair
Young boys made cards to Heaven to bring to their mom,
As we walked down the aisle, her song played.
Annie's song,
That song made people cry more, and more.

Always With You
by Cynthia Timoteo

God is always with you
But you can't even see
Don't be crying boohoo
Because He will never leave.

Hershey Park
by Riana Ferrell

A water park with the water splashing everywhere,
I also saw the chocolate factory with the yummy kisses on top,
It make me just want to go running up there.
People yelling for their lives,
I can also hear people screaming for joy,
That sounded like they were having the best day of their lives,
Do you know the next thing I heard?
Well, I heard people laughing and having a great time.
The hot, milky, chocolate kisses in my mouth, moving side to side,
It was very chocolaty
The chocolate kisses coming from the chocolate factory,
I know that this is the most wonderful time in my whole life.

Where Can It Be?
by Allyssa Bollmann

Sitting there
Thinking, thinking
Saying to myself
Where, where
Can it be
Sure to that move
Yes I found the piece one the
Game

Spring
by Dashyra Ortiz

When flowers bloom, you feel so free.
It lets you be who you want to be.
Rich or poor, go outdoors
You'll feel better to go explore.
The light that shines above your head
Will not give you any thread.
The stronger you get, you won't get upset
When you go and see that beautiful sparkle.
That clean green grass, the blue ocean
All shows a sign, a sign that has spoken.
The beautiful butterflies, the peeping birds, the children showing their expression.
That beautiful sun, that brings in the fun, and the children who love to run.
They hear the ice cream truck.
They're in a rush.
The hot temperature was a lot for me.
That spring was the best for me.

All About Me
by Chelsea Greene

Chelsea Greene
Keep my BFF's forever
Never let anyone be the boss of me
Loves to sing and play ping pong
Krista Dong is one of my best friends
Also Richa Navalukar is one too
My favorite color is baby blue

A Woman's Independence Day
by Valery Tarco

Roses are red, violets are blue, so why am I so scared of you?
Is it because your eyes were red when you said never again?
Or maybe 'cause you're always there sitting on my tall blue chair.
I see you go out at night and meet some people there.
I know you're planning something bad and wonder why I care.
I love you, that's the reason.
But I do not know why I do.
'Cause you don't love me anyways, even though you say you do.
If you loved me, you wouldn't drink.
You wouldn't hit and yell, you'd treat me like a woman, you would treat me well.
I don't know how this happened or why I fell for you.
I only know the things that show.
Obviously it's much more than you think.
But you do not think at all.
For if you did, you'd love me and stare at me in awe.
For you'd know what you have done to me.
And you will rue that very day. For that's the day I'll leave you.
That will be my independence day.

Dreams
by Nicole Strus

Think about the times we spent together
We were there forever,
We were young
Forget about the fights we ever had
Dreams do come true as long as you're true to them
Then if you're true to them you'll never fight again
Forget about the fights we ever had
Dreams do come true as long as you're true to them
Then if you're true to them you'll never fight again
Dreams come true
Dreams come true
Stay true

I Just Can't Wait Till Friday
by Laura Allen

I can't wait till Friday
Friday, I say
Forty-eight more hours
I will dance till my feet ache
I will sing till I'm out of breath
I just can't wait till Friday
I will dance three hours non-stop
I will listen to three songs
Jail House Rock
Start the Party
We're In the Money
I just can't wait till Friday
I get to see my friends
I just can't wait till Friday

Strawberries
by Kylie George

Strawberries, strawberries,
So juicy and red.
I really love to eat them in bed.
Strawberries, strawberries,
They're the color of my heart,
You can eat them plain, or bake them in a tart.
Strawberries, strawberries,
They go great with chocolate,
But be careful, because they'll melt in your pocket.
Strawberries, strawberries,
They're my favorite food,
They put me in a really great mood!

Precious Purple
by Precious Njokubi

The color purple looks like a dress
That's full of beauty, grace, elegance, and romance.
That's what it looks like to me.
The color purple sounds like purple trumpets of royalty,
A loud sound of justice.
That's what it sounds like to me.
The color purple tastes like grapes from a nearby vine.
So delicious ... yum!
That's what it tastes like to me.
The color purple smells like violets that smell really pretty.
That heavenly aroma ... smelling so sweet.
That what it smells like to me.
So, the next time you think of a color,
Think, and feel free to write what it means to you.
That's a reminder from me!

Golden Eggs
by Madison Vitale

As the family gathers, golden eggs fill the yard,
I warn my cousins that the hunt will be hard.
Easter eggs and candy galore,
There's a golden egg full of money and more.
There's gumdrops, and gum, and lollypops too!
There's another golden egg, one of a few.
A golden egg shines bright in the sun,
Charging towards it couldn't be more fun.
I find a golden egg in the bark of a tree,
I shout to the world, "That one's for me!"
There's a glistening flower—wait, that's not right,
It's a golden egg that catches my sight!
My bag's almost full; I almost have ten,
Where did these come from? A magical hen?
As I sprinkle some water to my face from the hose,
I feel a golden egg with my soaking wet toes.
I grab it and run, as fast as I can;
The egg hunt is over! I found ten!

If I Were the Queen Cat
by Joy Anderson

If I were the queen cat
I would catch fish everyday.
I would own a fast moving ball and seven kittens.
I would help the homeless animals even mice,
And give them a blanket out of my fur.
I would make sure every animal had food and shelter.
I would make a law that cats and mice could be friends
If I were the queen cat.

My Orange Kite
by Nina Borja

I have an orange kite soaring through the sky,
This is no doubt and no lie.
This orange kite is very special and dear
That it doesn't have a single scratch or smear.
To me, this toy is number one!
I will never stop flying this kite, and be done.
To you, this may seem to be an ordinary kite,
But, to me, it is a gift of life,
So, whenever you pass by the park, you'll always see a little kid flying her kite
With its tail ready for its flight!

There's No Pet Like Nemo
by Janet Martinez

You're not a dog, but you're a cat
You're not a fish, but you're named like that
You can scratch up the leather, you can feel like a blue feather
You can wake me up in the middle of the night
Because you're my cat and I leave it at that
The cat that's a cute, loving sight.

Without the Tree, Where Would We Be?
by Edward Gomez

Where would we be without the tree?
Bees make hives upon it
We see the bird without a word
Making its nest to fit
Where would we be without the tree?
Squirrels jumping from limb to limb
They never fall, they have a ball
Like a personal jungle gym
Where would we be without the tree?
Leaves rustle in the breeze
Everyone can stay in its shade
Unless you have allergies

My Dog Meghan
by Anthony Olizi

Running like a cheetah around the house.
Bumping, pushing, knocking down everything in her path.
Licking, kissing, my face gets all wet.
Sometimes it looks like I'm in a pool but it's really just my pet.
I love my dog Meghan, even though she's so big.
She's the best German Shepard a kid can ever get

Baseball
by Tyler Hering

Be a good sport
Always be a good teammate
Stealing bases is cool
Extra innings are fun
Be a good hitter
Always try your best
Losing's not much fun
Love the game of baseball

My Sister
by Ron'Renier Gavin

Runs in a circle a lot
Happy most of the time
Yaps all the time
Artistically good

Fun to talk to
Really funny
Annoying when it comes to talking
Not shy at all
Colors in her book a lot
Every kind of animal is her favorite
Super duper special

Good at drawing animals
Always gets her way
Very stubborn
Insect lover as well
Needs attention a lot

Spring
by Lydia Schustermann

Spring is beautiful
Planting everywhere
Rain falling from the sky
In the ground, flowers are planted
No flower isn't blooming
Great birds in the sky

Earth Day
by Haeleigh Cocco

Everyone should appreciate
And care for the Earth.
Remember to recycle and save energy.
To preserve a
Healthy community,

Don't use too much water
And clean up litter so
You can live in a happy place.

Spring Is Here
by Siera Meaux

Spring is here
Pie in the spring
Ready to go
Ice pops ready
New things
Growing flowers

Earth
by Alexa Porcelli

Everyone should clean up
Animals need to stay healthy
Reduce, reuse, and recycle
The weather needs to be better
Help the Earth stay clean

Spring
by Rushil Garala

School almost out
Popsicles finally bought
Riding your bike
Ice cream truck going around town
New flowers blossoming
Going outside to play with everyone

Minnesota
by Skyler Fleisher

Mall of America is there!
Inline skates were developed in Minnesota.
Nicknamed the North Star state.
Norway pine is the tree.
Environment is great: it has birds, animals, fish, trees, and more!
Split Rock Lighthouse guides ships along Lake Superior's rocky shores.
Onions are one of the main agricultural products.
There are over five hundred stores in the Mall of
America, in Bloomington, Minnesota!

Summertime
by Michael Tom

Summer is coming soon!
Ultra-tasty ice cream in different flavors
Many people will go swimming
Munching on food
Extra fun!
Running all around
Time to have fun
Ice cream is delicious
Many kids are playing
Exiting school

Celtics
by Hannah Barnett

Cool
Entertaining to watch
Love basketball
Talented
Incredible
Can't compare to other teams
Shocking

Escape
by Nahdiyyah Hogue

Where can I escape
Like escaping from a jail
Sail with one plastic spoon or the steal bars.
My feelings are bursting out of me
But my crying holds it back,
As if rain was falling on an umbrella blocking your face.
I cry more than the storm on April 20, 2009
Even though my heart seals it up after one day.
Where can I escape,
Not into today or into yesterday.

How Beautiful Is My Mom
by Justin Martin

She is so pretty
I love her very much
She is the most beautiful girl in the world
And she's a good cook

School
by Darlyn Miranda

School is so fun
I meet all my friends and we get all along.
I learn too much.
Math, Writing, Reading is not that much fun,
But when I get to lunch it's number 1.
Recess is fun.
I play Uno and tag.
It's fun to play and run.
Then all I got to do is finish school
Become famous and you will know me too!

Class
by Madison McGovern

I like it in class
With so much to do
Math, science, and history too
Learning, subtraction, and how to add a number
And in social studies, learning about Michigan's lumber
But the best thing of all, when all your work is done
Is having a friend to double the fun

Mold
by Patrick Brady

Mold ...Yuck!
Mold ... Ew!
Mold ... I can't think of anything else!

3rd Place

Abraham Fakhreddine

Abraham was in the fifth grade
when he wrote his award-winning poem.
Creativity is obviously his strong suit,
and we hope he continues to cultivate his talent.

Feel My Rhythm
by Abraham Fakhreddine

I am poetry
There is meaning in my every word.
I am full of inspiration
When you need me,
Just take me in your arms
And feel the rhythm I contain.
I may soothe you and comfort you
Or I may make you angry and enrage you.
No matter what happens, hold me tight
And drift into the flow of me
Rhythmic feelings.

2nd Place

Anusha Bishop

Anusha lets her serious side show
with her entry in this year's student poetry contest.
"I Am the Dark" is quite advanced writing
and a very impressive offering.

I Am the Dark
by Anusha Bishop

I am the dark
My voice is hidden in the shadows
A black cloak keeps my thoughts from entering the world
I am unfathomable
Not able to show who I am and what I can do
Sometimes a bright moon pierces the clouds surrounding me
And lets me shine
But that is not enough
Because I will always prevail
I am the dark

1st Place

Fiona Cohen

Fiona is looking forward
to turning twelve in the new year,
and in her spare time enjoys
writing, drawing, and learning a new instrument.
She hopes one day to become
an interior designer
or perhaps an artist.

I Think I Can't
by Fiona Cohen

I am the Little Engine That Couldn't
You say that I can do it
You say I have to try
You say I have to think I can
Well I can't
It's not that easy
The mountain lies ahead
Suggesting in its own quiet way
That I should go back
To where I came from
Just turn around
Take the easy way out
Avoid the towering mountain
Stay the Little Engine That Couldn't

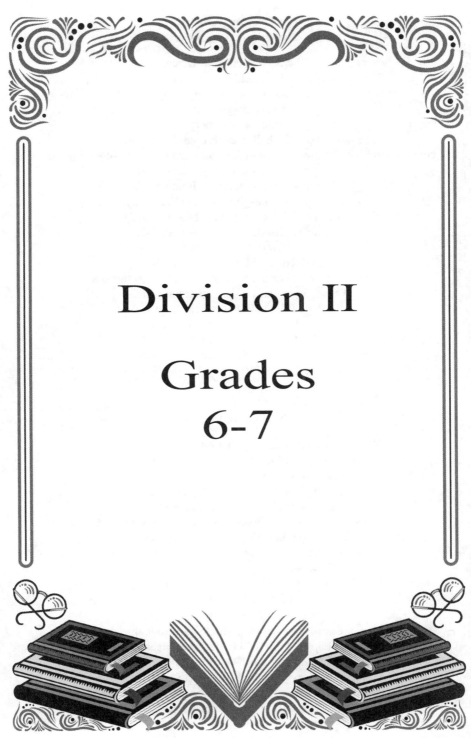

Division II

Grades
6-7

Everything Counts
by Megan Dougherty

Today, we verse our rivals,
Quite possibly the best field hockey players in the state,
And right now, we will do anything to win.
Everything counts.
I am a defender;
The last person the ball goes through before the goal.
My coach say to dive, do anything to make sure that ball does not get into the goal.
As the game starts the ball comes toward me;
And the girl carrying it drives it into my knee.
I ignore the pain as the foul is called on her,
And I drive it back towards their defenders.
After half time, the score is tied: 2-2.
Everything counts.
Suddenly, with two minuets left,
Their offense and our defense in a strait line on the goal.
Our offense can't do anything but watch.
One little fault and it is all over.
And that's what lost us the game.
That day we learned yet again,
Everything counts.

Celebrate Earth Day
by Valentina Valencia

We all come together on Earth Day
As we all have a few words to say
Earth is our home, our place to live
Yet there is only so much this planet can give
Water, warmth, energy, shelter, and food!
Plus there's more, no wonder Earth is in a bad mood
We use too much energy, too many resources
We're driving Earth around in so many courses
Yet there are so many ways to save
To return the favor to Earth for what she gave
Like turn off the sink while not in use
And make sure the sink is not loose
Because, when your sink begins to leak
Earth's faith in help becomes bleak
You can also buy Earth-friendly bulbs for light
This way you don't give Earth a fright
Start today, you can help Earth–there are so many ways!
You can start by celebrating Earth Day!

When All Is Calm
by Catherine Liberio

At the end of the day
The sky seems to sway like the rushing waters of the roughly moving ocean.
I can almost string my fingers through the gentle, streaming clouds
The trees brush, whispering
Releasing feather light, emerald green leaves
To the lush grass underneath
The velvety petals start to tuck away
Going to sleep for a brand new day
Mother Nature has blown a gust of howling wind
Spitting calm, tangerine lava like clouds into the briskly sky
The warm husky blue melts away fading into night
Stars begin to appear and glisten brightly in their own unique way
Shhh ...
If you listen closely, you can hear the roar of the galaxies above
And the twinkle of the plentiful stars overhead
Just beyond the sunset
Someone waits for me
Just beyond the sunset
Lies my destiny

Architecture
by Isabella Petrossian

Driving.
New York City.
Skyscrapers, churches, and antiques galore.
I think: everything and anything has beauty.
I can't stop thinking-or staring.
I wonder about the past.
How were these buildings used in the past?
I want to get my camera, but I'm in a trance.
I want to reach out to the beauty.
I seem to be dozing off, but it's against my will.
I think about what my friends would say: would they agree?
Would they think I was crazy?
But I'm not.
Anyone can see the beauty, if they tried.
But everyone's too busy thinking about our new, modern world.
My mind seems cleansed, fresh.
I have something to think about.
It's miraculous. It's wonderful. It's man made art.
My mind whirrs with possible questions.
It's unexplainable beauty with the power to touch anyone.

Spring Is the New Thing
by Taylor Biasco

Spring is the new thing.
The warm weather is in.
Bright colors, like violet, pink, yellow,
Green, orange, and light blue.
Friends are there to care.
Almost no school.
Swimming, tanning, ice cream,
And the best of all, new lives being born.

My Saviors
by Kevin Morgan

Marines, you are the saviors and protectors of my life.
All day, you battle in an everlasting strife.
You're everything I expect.
You have all my respect.
You are in so many wars.
Jumping out of floors.
You have no fears.
Dodging bullets and spears.
Riding around in submarines,
You are the great Marines.
You charge into buildings,
Saying your famous phrase, "Ooh Rah!"

Ode To My Microwave
by Benjamin Gillo

Thank you, microwave
You make any food I crave
You make my food really good
You make making food so it could be understood
Mr. Microwave, you made food for my Uncle Dave
He says thank you for making every food he'd crave
You always make food very good
So when you're broken, go under your hood
Thank you, Mr. Microwave
For making food I crave

Spring
by Erin Sassaman

Children swimming in the pool
Trying to keep cool
Trips to the beach
Staying healthy by eating a peach
Doing yard work
Having a picnic with pulled pork
Birds chirp and bells ring
Yippee! It's spring!

Words
by Alexa Smyth

Words, dripping from the mouth of forget and grief
Something said, something lost, never to be retrieved,
Go as swiftly as set free
Words, spoken softly, the greatest fear
Sent away to the alley of loneliness, eaten by loss, forgotten so soon
Something said, never gained, words spoken, never taken
Bauble, gobble, a constant dribble of muck
Sprayed so mindlessly, meaninglessly, colorlessly
From the pit of tasteless mud
Be careful what you say, it could damage more then one
Words: see them go, hear them hurt, watch them seep
Words, never to be retrieved

School
by Aashka Barot

Okay, I agree school is cool,
Even without a swimming pool!
Teachers read books about creatures,
Doesn't my school have a lot of features!
My music teacher is a mean, green, singing machine,
Basically she's an extreme!
Chewed gum pieces are stuck on the fountains,
Mostly the gums look like mountains!
I told you enough about school,
So don't be a fool that breaks the rule!
Just go to school!

Spring
by Felicia Krysa

The sun shines bright on all the flowers,
It does this for many long hours.
The grass is so tall and green,
That makes it look very clean.
Some trees can be small,
Others are very tall.
Some mountains are very high,
Others are not tall enough to touch the sky.
The clouds look so fluffy and white,
I am sure they are very light.
The sky is high and blue,
It looks shiny and new.

Puppies
by Julia McClure

Puppies are small.
Puppies are cute.
They run around all day.
Then, they curl up into a ball and take a nap.

My Imaginary Place
by Didier Louis

In this special place I explore on my own
I see the water splashing against my face
I hear the kids screaming and yelling
I smell hot dogs floating in the air
I touch the sand spreading away on my hands
I taste the chocolate bar melting in my mouth
I see the waves overlapping
I hear the wind blowing faster
I see a families' picnics flying all over the place
I hear the families gathering their things
I still smell the leftover hot dogs floating in the air
I touch my stomach to feel it growl
I taste the leftover chocolate in my mouth
I now see everyone leaving
I stand in the middle of the beach
Just me and my five senses

Cocoa
by Amy Bergen

Just like the cold winter potion
Cocoa is sweet
Cocoa is dark
Cocoa is warm
Just like a spinning motion
Cocoa is quick
Cocoa can jump
Cocoa runs
Just like true devotion
Cocoa needs me
Cocoa knows I need her
Cocoa loves Amy

The Storm
by Sophia Morong

The wind whistles,
With the dancing leaves.
Little rain boots splash in puddles.
Rain squirms, falling from the sky,
A storm is coming.

Basketball
by Michelle Metcalf

Tirelessly I slide
Across the rink that is twice as long
As it is wide
Toward one of the goals
That lies at either end
And against which my opponent
Is helpless to defend
Gracefully I glide
Like a hawk through the sky toward the prey
I'm the hawk eye
She thinks she will score,
But she has no more chance than a mouse
Fleeing across the forest floor.

Ice Cream
by Andrew Ciallella

Mint chocolaty
Icky sticky creamy
Makes you refreshed in the hot summer
I love ice cream
Delicious Oreo, yummy fudge
Gooey gummy bears, Reese's pieces
Makes your ice cream better
I love ice cream
Waffle cones, pretzel cones
Colorful sprinkle cones, sugar cones
Makes your ice cream the best
I love ice cream
Dripping on the floor cold and tasty
Falling on the pavement tastes like Heaven
Makes your hands sticky
So many flavors
But, we still love our ice cream!

Life
by Jaspreet Kaur

Life is a challenge
Life without challenge is bleak
Life is enjoyment
Life without enjoyment is dull
Life is full of light
Life without light is black
Life is miserable
Life without misery is never possible
Life is surprise
Life without surprise is horrible
Life is suspense
Life without suspense is suspicious
Life is adventure
Life without adventure is adverse
Life is affection
Life without affection is affliction
Life is blossom
Life without blossom is a burden
At last, life is life
Life without life is death

English
by Stephanie Guzmán

What a besotted language we speak
Orthography so very muddled
Letters prancing around raucously
People resorting to mnemonic tricks
For recalling cantankerous words
How do you spell "cnemial," "pneumatic," or "gnome"?
Where does the double "a" go in Afrikaans?
How do you diagnose psoriasis?
Minute words, monstrous words
Plain words, perplexing words
Silent letters, spoken letters
Will immense meet infinitesimal at a compromise?
A rendezvous point?
Yes, the English language is an intricate one
No rules that work all the time
Words and weird words
Words and weirder words
I'll stop now
I'm giving myself
Hippopotomonstrosesquippedaliophobia

Hard To Get Friend
by Renzo Eseo

As I pressed down to roll my window, a sign caught my eyes
"Garage Sale at: 5 Millsberry Street
Be there at 4:00-6:00 PM
Don't be late!"
I grasped the toys and "knick-and-knacks"
Old pots, games, and more ...
But ...
There was one thing I couldn't get my eyes off!
I studied, and checked it, and looked at its button eyes;
Its perfectly combed, nice coat of faded brown fuzz ...
Oh, wait ... I forgot something so important!
Money ... Hard-to-get, green money
I looked at it in despair
Its green button eyes staring at me ... Wanting to be cared for
Destiny, love, and joy
A friend I couldn't get
How horrible!

Ode To Joy
by Nathan Merino

Joy is an emotion like no other
Joy is the colors of the rainbow
Joy is the smell of cinnamon and mint
Joy is the taste of sweet vanilla ice cream
Joy is the sound of the robins in spring, chirping for company
Joy is the feel of soft, warm cotton
Joy is an emotion like no other
Joy differs for all of us
Maybe money, or the beach, but everyone shares the same feeling
Cherished, celebrated
Joy is an emotion like no other.

Untitled
by Laura Fraser

The water stands still as the sun rises.
Its colors bleeding in the sky.
The lake reflects the colors of the sky–magenta
And the trees and the leaves sway
And communicates in a way that is foreign to us.
The water stands peaceful, proud, and somehow glorious.
The beauty of the lake is breathtaking,
I love it here.

Seashell
by David Fefer

I found a seashell in the sea,
Blue and shiny as it could be.
I found it on the shore one day,
Somewhere close to Sheepshead Bay.
In a little bag it fit,
Having the sea sound inside of it.
I put it in a little frame,
And planned to sell it when the time came.
I planned to sell it for a buck,
But they said to keep it, for good luck.
I decided to take their wise advice,
And kept it, always clean and nice.
For now my life's gone very well,
Thanks to that little, blue, shiny shell.

When I Go
by Alexa Derman

Sometimes I go to a doctor,
But not often, not usually.
Silly to spend money on a dying girl.
No one will say it,
But I know it, I feel it.
He always denies it, more to himself than me,
But I hear my internal clock, counting down my days.
I want to go amongst my friends, with my love,
Not on a hospital bed, in a room that smells like disease
I want to go holding a single, lit candle
Not a bottle of AZT.
I want to go, young and in love,
Smiling towards the light,
And unafraid

Summer
by Nicole Ciuppa

I've been anxiously longing for the coming of summer
All this waiting was a bummer
Now that it's here I'm ready to play
And be sure to lay in the sun all day
Going to the beach will be fun
So I can jump, splash, and swim in the sun
Skim-boarding will be fun too
Now I know these are facts that are true

Fridays Are the Best!
by Christina Lee

Fridays are the best and the last days of school.
Having fun like all children do.
Free! Free! Free! I do want to say!
But the end is near! That is what adults say!
Working! Working! Working! That is what everybody agrees!
Mondays through Fridays are all school days!
Working is fun, for all children say!
Work! Work! Work! Is not my name!
I do love working and participate as a learner!
Sometimes I just wish I can take a break again!

Fire
by Elisa Costanza

Slowly watching everything of your childhood go by
Dying in a fire
Your whole life going past
Too fast, too fast
Trying to catch it
But it's too strong, and you let go
Let go of everything
Everything you ever loved
Now you are standing in the middle of nowhere
Not knowing what to do
What to say
The whole world is blank now
I could have done better, much better
But now, for my foolish mistake
I made everything I ever had
Go up in four walls of fire
Not letting me out
Not letting me speak
Not letting me get out of this little room of death.

War
by Jon Paul Barry

War is our way of solving big problems
The way of solving freedom, peace, and rights
There are many "bumps" in the world's road
War is our way of repairing them
Peace, rights, and freedom are all big bumps
As you may know, people have been fighting for a long time
With war, comes peace
And peace will turn to war
Peace: a thing the world wishes for
But, in my eyes, the world will never seek this thing we call "world peace"
Peace is only temporary
It comes and goes
It is found and it is lost
We can only gain this temporary peace with ... War

Dads That Are Here and Away
by Raymond Marshall

Sometimes I go, sometimes I stay
I will never forget that day
The fathers that are here
Maybe you can hear
I can be a better man
And maybe a better friend
Just spend a day with your son
Maybe you can come
We can go to the mall
And play a lot of ball
Dads that are gone
You are missing a lot of fun
It don't cost a thing to remain
Please don't complain
Family is home
Not alone
Love your kids
For who they is
Sometimes I go, sometimes I stay
I will never forget that day

Why?
by Malachi Robinson

Why do I even try
Try to impress people?
Try to fit in?
But I wonder if I was born to stand out
I live my life doing things different
Different from everybody else
But, then, I see people trying to be like me
I feel good about that
But, then, I think, "Are they serious?"
You never really know with people today
Who is real and who is fake
But then I ask why?
Why?

Nature
by Yeriel Castillo

Nature is like a living spirit,
Where there is a lot of love in it.
Nature is in the Earth,
And has been there from birth.
Nature is like a rhyme,
That doesn't waste your time.
Nature is like a song,
That remains for so long.
Nature lets us free to live,
Because there is air to breathe.
Nature is all over the world,
And it's sometimes shaped as a swirl.
Nature is in the air,
When you're not aware.
Nature makes the Earth's beauty,
While you are on duty.
Nature is a flower,
That gives us power.
Nature is like a song,
That makes the Earth strong.

A Silent Prayer
by Zaria Steward

He's always there, always by your side, but never seen
How can this be, you ask
How can he be there, but never seen?
Who is this person who is never seen?
This person is your Creator
He's the One who gave you life
His name means Father, His name means Emmanuel
But His most important name is "I Am"
Who is "I Am," you ask?
"I Am" is the Mighty One
Who is "I Am" to us?
"I am" is the One who is never seen
But is ever-present
He is your Silent Prayer.

Adventure
by Sarah Sleiman

As the birds peep,
I seek
An adventure that is waiting
For you and me.
We decide
Which side
To take.
They are both waiting to meet,
Take your time,
Don't just glide,
But be ready
For an adventure that is steep.

Goodbye
by Ashley Clemons Miller

Roses are red, violets are blue
We were a class that suddenly passed.
Our memories flew as we said goodbye
We shed a tear; it was our final goodbye!
We've been together forever in time,
And now it's the end, as we wave bye-bye!
We had our ups and downs, our rounds and rounds,
We'll be together forever in time.
When we say goodbye, it won't descend,
Our friendship is strong; it will never end!

What Is a Poem?
by Alyssa Rodriguez

What is a poem? What can it be?
Thinking of this is filling me with glee!
A poem is a story, a phrase, a folk tale.
It can be about anything, anybody, female or male.
A poem can be scary, ridiculous, and fun.
You can write it, act it, say it, or just keep it mum.
So, you see that poems are wonderful and poems are so great.
So, enjoy them with your friends and all of your mates.

Disappearance
by Michael Szegedy

Here, in the woodlands,
Which once was home
To birds, who soared above
Worms, who tunneled below
And deer, who skipped gracefully through shrubs,
Leaves are wilting
Willows drooping
Even soil feels without purpose
Since it got warm.
They left, seeking cold
So now, the stream feels tired
Of running all day.
Dull rocks are soft
Once swift winds, still
Rain, dry
And snow no longer falls
But lingers in the clouds
Who have left the lifeless skies long ago
In need of air that has not been tainted
With the taste of humanity.

Marching Through Fire
by Dylan Lambe

They've opened up fire, but we fought through the flames
Pushed all the way through all the loss and the pain
Our soldiers are circled in the war's bloodthirsty wrath
As we try to escape, death lets out his laugh
Buildings are burning; you know hundreds are dead
When the this war's finally over, it'll still be in my head
The bullets keep flying as they shred through our pride
We keep on fighting 'cause our souls have not died
From land to sea we go, testing our strength
They needed protection, and we walked the length
As we watch our friends die, we hold back our tears
Hoping and praying for a large number of years
The bodies keep dropping, the hatred still flying
Throughout this country, the families are crying
If we win this war, it'll be at what cost?
I stay and I fight, but my mind is so lost.

Stand Tall
by Kari Shankle

Through the sky, I will soar
While the wind will roar
The sun on my wings
As I fly
To the Pacific
To the Atlantic
Through fields and fields
Where tulips bloom
To a wide open range
Where I will zoom
Through perilous mountains
And treacherous terrain
People will say
"It won't be safe!"
But I will test danger
And I will test fate
Can you believe people call me small?
But I will prove them wrong
And show them that even the smallest
Can stand tall

Family
by Nyeira Webb

My family helps me to be the best I can be,
The star that shines with a light on me;
We love each other each day and night,
My family gives me hope and it feels so right;
Family is everything, your ups and downs,
They give you love every day, whenever you're feeling down.
Family teaches us how to grow up strong,
And live the life the right way, so our years last long;
Family is the Bible because we all have one
I thank God for my family and all He has done;
Families barbecue on a hot summer day,
On Sundays they go to church, love God, and pray;
Family is my all, and they love me everyday
And I love my family back, and feel the same way.

First Crush
by Cibely Leguizamon

I never noticed you
When we saw each other in the hallways
You would smile and I would look down
And I would look back to you and smile
My friends said you had a crush on me
Of course, I never believed them
Until, one day, you messaged me; you said I was beautiful
I couldn't believe what I was reading as you said you had a crush on me
I was never sure if I liked someone as much as you liked me
My friends teased me about you liking me
As the days went on, all the teasing made me think twice
You asked me to the dance, I didn't know what to say
We went to the dance somewhat together, but we didn't even dance
Sometimes, at night, I think of you, and I take a deep breath,
I think of my first love and you are the first thing to come to mind
I smile and think that, for the first time, I had a true crush
I had denied your love, and now I regret that
I don't think you will accept me after what I caused your heart to go through
But I won't beg, I will be patient until you notice me once more
Just like the first day you said you liked me ...

Ode To the Beach
by Delphine Uriburu

"And we're off!" said Mom,
All three of us packed in our Subaru,
Loving every moment of it
We were going to my favorite place on Earth:
The beach!
The second we got there,
I could feel the soft breeze blowing against my body,
The sand molding the shape of my feet
I could hear the low crashing of the waves in the distance,
Relaxing me into a nearly mellow, subconscious state,
Like when soft raindrops fall on a windowpane
Sweet humming laughter arose in the air
And soon, it became contagious
Many images flashed before our eyes, like blinking strobe lights
The sun glistened down on the ocean,
Like fireflies sparkling in the dead of night.
The dolphins splashed in the water
Playing like three-year-olds with bubbles
And I was there, enjoying every minute of it

The Night Sky
by David Han

When the sun sets, and the moon rises,
When the stars appear winking at us,
We see before us the night sky.
So big, yet so small, so dim yet so clear,
The moon and its unblinking light shines on us
Little specks of light shining like glitter,
Enhancing the beauty of the sky at night
Forming constellations are stars.
Vast, deep, dark, and empty.
Cold, black space dominates the night,
Giving off no light, it looms above us,
And fills in the gaps between the moon and stars.

Trees
by Mary Clare Foley

Green, brown, and ancient
Lose their leaves in the winter
But not evergreens
Always still, quiet, and peaceful
There are different shapes and types

Oh, How I Love Spring
by Evelyn Morales

I love spring
It makes me sing
Birds, flowers
And the April showers
All I hate are the allergies
They take away all the glee
But forget all the negative
I'll just focus on the positive
April, March, and May
Oh, how I love those days!
Put away that winter coat
And jump into a nice boat
Vacation's here
The class all cheers
All the happiness it brings
Oh, how I love spring!

Spring
by Nicole Sanchez

Today, I woke up to something in the air
The sound of birds caught my ear
Chirp, chirp, the birds' song
I bend over the window
And, to my surprise, what do I see?
Flowers and buds
And, well, everything!
But what can I say?
That's spring, my friend!

Need
by Lenine Lasher

Like a cup of coffee needs half and half
Like a balloon needs air
Like a woman needs shoes
Like a table needs chairs
Like a sleeper needs a bed
Is like the way I need you.

Summertime
by Victoria Waller

People lying on the beach,
As if it was a dream.
While children are eating a peach,
And others prefer delicious ice cream.
Sweat pours down my face,
As I jump into the pool.
We have a swimming race,
But, hopefully, I don't look like a fool.
Riding my bike down the street,
Going with my friends,
Riding with bare feet,
Hopefully my feet don't bend!
Now it is the end of our summertime,
This time will come again.
See you next time!
My beautiful summertime.

Lily Queen
by Julia Kornick

Boating on a lake, one peaceful day's morn.
I spot a white flower, which was battered and torn.
Drifting in a lake carelessly, dripping with silver beads,
Broken sunbeams spewing out, like the light on which it feeds.
A maiden dressed in a silk white gown, with pearls draped over her,
Delicate as a butterfly, though perhaps even more pure,
Splattered with golden spots, glowing as queen of the pond.
Her emerald throne gleaming, on which she sings her song.
So fine it can match an ocean breeze that whistles through your hair.
Ripples bouncing off of her, despite the damage that she wears.
The only flower on the water, far as the eye can see.
Circles spinning off our boat, touching her, then touching me.

What You Are
by Olivia Harwick

You are my friend.
You are my sister/brother.
You are my companion.
You are my promise.
You are the light in my dark.
You are the wish in my star.
You are the warmth in my hug.
You are the color in my rainbow.

Me, Us, Soccer
by Kyle Kristiansen

My heart's in the game, followed by my head and soul
When I'm on the field, I will never get old
I kick and I run till I'm caked with dirt
Sweat flowing from my brows that I will wipe off with my shirt
There is so much going on, like whether to dribble or pass
It floods my mind like an intricate task
No one can elude us; we are a deft force
We score all the time; we won't be coerced
This possessing game we play cannot be mocked by the world's greatest mocker
Because this magical way of life is found in a sport called soccer.

A Random Act of Kindness ...
by Robert Piper

I am that homeless man you see every day
With nothing to keep warm
I am that little girl who's been abandoned
With clothes that are tattered and torn
I know, to you, I don't mean much
But, please, toss a coin my way
Heed my words, please, listen closely
To what I have to say
A small act of random kindness
Can end up changing the world, you see
And it releases your inner beauty
For all the world to see
Right now, I might just be a lonesome man
Sitting in the gutter
But, tomorrow, I could be more beautiful than
A butterfly starting to flutter
Kindness is a universal language
Regardless of your religion or race
When everyone is full of kindness
The world truly is a better place
You must be the change you wish to see
So, why not start with helping me?

Dogs
by Kevin Jackson

A dog is the greatest pet,
And no matter what, I'll bet,
That your love will never end,
Because he's man's best friend.
Whether you scratch his back or throw a ball,
He'll always be there when you call.
If you're on the couch, he'll lick your feet,
But that might just mean he wants to eat.
He'll scare the mailman, or chase the cat,
Or sometimes, he'll just lie on a mat.
Whether playing with him in the spring or fall,
Having a dog is the greatest of all.

My Pain
by Sheel Patel

It feels as if there is a hole in my chest that grows and grows, rather than shrinks.
Like thousands and thousands of screams are surrounding me.
Like everything in the world is crashing down on me.
This is my pain, the pain that will never go away.

Who Is That?
by Victoria Martinez

Who is that girl?
The one looking back at me
I feel as if I've known her my whole life
We are so alike
Yet so different
She is always there
We are like best friends
But also like enemies
We put our hands to our heart
Then by our side
I look away from her
And I look at her again
I raise my hand to touch her as she does the same
I touch her and then back away
As I realize,
That girl ...
She is me!

Live Like a Jellyfish
by Leanne Skibicki

Live like a jellyfish.
Go with the flow.
What will happen, you'll never know.
Live like a jellyfish.
Don't use your eyes.
Think about things more and you'll be surprised.
Live like a jellyfish.
Glow and shine.
Always do your best, and you'll have a great time.
Live like a jellyfish.
Enjoy all your average days.
On second thought, just follow my advice, jellyfish don't have brains.

Spending Blues
by Johnathan Apuzen

Another recession has come our way
Now is the time people have to repay
Most of us simply use credit cards
To charge for the things in our shopping carts
All we're doing is building up debt
Yet, saving money is our best bet
Keeping your job is a good idea too
Not like that's anything new
And all you kids that ask for PSP's
Pretend you're a mother, would you please?
I really don't think the President's to blame
He shouldn't be the one in shame
As you can see, the economy's in a tumble
So, make sure you're spending doesn't cause more trouble.

A Special Place
by Amanda Davis

I need a place to live my dreams,
To be who I really wish to be.
A place to live my life with no regrets,
To be myself and have no frets.
I need a place to think about life.
Consider my thoughts and be just right.
This place I need does not exist.
This place I need is just for me.

Tweet!
by Claire Cowan

The chirp of birds is sacred,
One of the only other languages that we hear.
All birds,
From noisy crows to hummingbirds,
Talk almost all year,
They start when summer is near,
And end when winter is almost upon us.
Like the birds, some people are made to sing all year.

My Rough Day
by Brian Reyes

I wake up early in the morning and take a shower.
I go down to breakfast, but I don't eat
Because the bus is here
And I run as fast as I can to catch it.
I get to school very confident
But the confidence doesn't last long
Because they start calling me names.
I think I'm a loser, and they say I am, but I know I'm not.
My mom picks me up from school
In a rusty car that wouldn't last long
So we got as far as we could
But we had to walk until we finally got home.
I do my homework and then go to bed
But I decide to play instead.

I Appreciate My Dad In Every Way
by Alexander Plaza Jr.

I appreciate you, Dad,
You provide me with protection and affection,
And I appreciate that.
Sometimes it doesn't seem like I show it, but I do hold it,
I always say I love my dad, even if we fight or argue,
That's one of my ways of showing you appreciation.
When you yell, or talk to me about important things,
I understand that you are doing it because you care about me,
And I appreciate that.
You always talk to me about the things that I did wrong; you'd never hit me,
You tell me you don't want to be the type of dad who hits their kid,
And I appreciate that.
You would come for me as soon as you heard I got hurt, even if you had work,
And, of course, I appreciate that!
When I'm home by myself, you call me every ten to twenty minutes to check on me.
Agh! Sometimes that gets annoying,
But, Dad, I appreciate that.
Dad, I love you and you love me,
So Dad, just keep helping me,
And, just so you know, I appreciate you, Dad!

Ripples On the Sea
by Ryan Teehan

In the beginning, there were three
Rising voices, like the sea
But one rose above the rest
Sought and strove to be the best
Sang a tune of awful discord
As he fought to be the lord
Of those thoughts still unadorned
The void was torn between the three
Crashing voices, like waves upon the endless sea
Then there was a fourth
A gentle ripple that grew in size
To reach the moment of their demise
And becalmed the tides of time
With a rhyme, the world was born
In a time, the sky adorned
Then, the one stood out, forlorn
As he saw his creations, unadorned

School, School
by Joseph Tagliareni

School, school is good for your brain
The more you think, the more you're smart.
The more you're smart, the better you are
So think, think, think, think in school.

Seasons
by Nicole Picinich

There are four seasons in the year,
Each one bringing about its own cheer.
Winter, the season of glistening snow,
With the jolly old man and his cheerful "Ho-Ho!"
Spring begins with a few showers,
But at the end, we see all the pretty flowers.
Summer is all about hot and lazy days,
And watching fireworks with a gaze.
Fall brings us some frightful nights,
With witches, goblins, and spooky delights.

Sky's the Limit
by Matthew Calle

Chilling in the dark, night blue sky,
Freezing, but feels so nice, looking at the sky,
Letting the stars take my open spirit, releasing the goodness in me.
Gazing at the stars even took my mind away from concentration on my life
To concentration on the shiny, bright stars and beautiful sky,
Settling the final goals in my life,
After achieving the goals, I will again be in peace
With the beautiful, dark, shiny sky.

Change of Address
by Sourya Vemuri

Bess gave Tess
Gettysburg's Address
Which got told to Pony Express
And the mailman saw a "Change of Address"
By mistake, he went to the Loch Ness
Tess told Bess that there was an SOS
In case of an emergencies, please use Air Express

A Better Place
by Kayla Corriveau

Although I didn't really spend time with him, I still miss my papa, John
He was always happy and loving
One day, I saw him; he didn't look the same,
It was like there was someone else in his body; he didn't even know my name
Then, I heard my grammy and mom talking about Alzheimer's
In the beginning, I didn't know what it meant
So, I asked my dad; first, I was really mad
But then, I realized I should spend more time with him, while he's still around
One day the phone rang; it was my grammy
All of a sudden there were tears in my dad's eyes
I asked him what's wrong; he didn't answer
At Christmas, I asked where he was
My grammy told me he went to a Better Place

The Highway
by Kristian Vera

Driving down the highway, you see
The cars,
The trees,
The road,
The signs,
Then finally, your destination.

Snow
by John Zhang

The snow blows away, singing its song
As I walk, I wonder, where does snow belong?
It is cold, and the color is white
The blanket of winter shines bright light
Now I really do wonder, can it do it in the summer?
Fall, spring, can it snow at least a flutter
One speck of snow, fall from the sky?
And if it's impossible, I wonder, why?
This is my speculation, of the blanket of white
Shining through blizzards, reflecting bright light
Exposing the beauty of the coldest of seasons
It is snow, coming from the sky in pieces

Salute
by Emily McAvoy

Hands blistered.
Heart pounding.
Mind racing.
Nervous.
Will I remember the routine?
I better get at least a nine.
Breathe hard.
Breathe heavy.
I'm up.
Salute, music, dance, hop,
Leap, flip, split.
I'm in the moment,
In my own little world.
Last step.
Deep breath.
Salute.

Deserted Path
by Jennie Cuco

Where will it lead me?
Dead tress and clouds are all I see
As the sun sets, my dreams begin to follow
As I watch the wonderful fun-filled day come to an end
I will have to walk this path
But I am afraid of where it will lead me
What if it leads me to a unknown land
Filled with pain and devastation?
But, what if it leads me to my dream?
I will become the person that I feel I am destined to be
Saving lives of helpless animals
No one knows
But I will walk this path to find out.
All I will say is that nothing or no one,
Not even the scariest of places and obstacles
Will keep me away.

Homework
by Otto Euller

Homework, oh, homework
Go away
Don't ever come back, we say
If you do, we will chase you back again
Yes, now it's gone, gone forever
But wait ... what about projects?

Friendship
by Andrea Schelmety

Friends are two people that share a certain bond.
If you ask them certain questions, they will respond.
She'll keep you up all night just to chat.
She'll go in your house, and take this and that.
Friends are people you love to be with.
This is the truth, it is not a myth.
You'll have your ups and your downs.
But, friends are people you always want to be around.

Autumn
by Alyssa Valvano

Atmosphere is crisp
Leaves are falling to the ground
It's getting chilly

Emptiness
by Elena Arida

What happened
To the times when we danced to the boom box in my cramped room?
To the times we would sit in the booths at the diner and order "fox fingers"?
What happened
To the Christmas Eves, exchanging presents?
To rolling down the big hill in your backyard?
What happened to your dad, my second father?
His absence changed everything.
What happened to the phone calls, the emails?
What happened to the friendship that we once shared?
What happened to the memories?
Do they not matter anymore?
What happened to the times we used to say we'd be together forever?
What happened to you?
What happened to me?
What happened to all we used to be?

Riding a Horse
by Carly Skibinski

Riding a horse is like nothing else
It's fun, even by yourself
The thrill of it all
The stillness of it all
The joy of flying through the air
The feeling of the wind in your hair
It's fun being way up high
It's like you could reach the sky
The fun of riding with your friends ...
It's like nothing you can comprehend
Riding, for me, is just a dream
So it seems
But when I wake up, I see
That it is more than what even I could see.

Warm Feeling
by Angie Stefanides

Caring is helping someone with their homework,
Or taking the time to tell someone you love them.
Ever get that warm feeling?
When you pray for someone who is about to pass,
Or just talking to someone who is angry or upset.
Ever get that warm feeling?
When you stick up for your friends against the populars,
Or making sure your brother(s) or sister(s) are safe.
Ever get that warm feeling?
That warm feeling is knowing that you did something right,
That warm feeling is caring.

Grammy
by Mandy Winzenried

I stand here, not a tear in my eyes
I wish for one more day with her
I hope she's happy now, wherever she is
I hold my father and sister while they cry
I know I can't cry; she wouldn't want me to
So I stand strong, while I grieve in my own way
While I stare down at a casket with my grandmother in it
So now I stand here, not a tear in my eyes.

Black Summer
by Danielle Heaney

Thunder booms,
The lights crackle,
A silence occurs,
Now pure darkness.
The wind whips,
Lightning breaks the darkness.
Drip, drop, splash,
The rain comes down in puddles,
Frightened on my bed, my dog whines.

A Special Place
by Lara Repholz

On summer days, in unbearable heat,
There's a special place where my friend and I meet.
In front of her house, under shady trees,
We share countless memories.
And by her house stands a basketball net,
So special because that's where we met.
And there we've cried, or screamed, or swore,
And the other would listen; that's what friends are for.
We'll sit there talking until the dead of night,
Sharing jokes, stories, and cans of sprite.
And, when our parents call at the night's end,
I leave that place and say goodbye to my friend.
And this applies to spring, winter, and fall,
Staying out late until our parents call.
And, when we get home and turn out our light,
Hoping tomorrow will be warm and bright.
And, knowing that, despite all our fun,
The best of our times is yet to come.

Through the Washington Borough School District
by Kyle Starita

In the Borough, we start out at Taylor Street
Where the education truly can't be beat
We have Math and Social Studies
We make friends and lots of buddies
And the teachers make it fun for us all week!
Then Memorial will take us to sixth grade
Everyone can see the progress that we've made
You have paved the road before us
With all the things you've taught us
So, now, raise your voices as we hear you say!
If you are a Borough Bear, now shout "Hooray!"
If you are a Borough Bear, now shout "Hooray!"
With our banners flying high
Blue and White across the sky
If you are a Borough Bear, now shout "Hooray!" (Hooray)

There For Me
by Dennise Reyes

When I open my eyes
I see the bright eyes
Of the person there for me
No matter what trouble
They will be there for me
Whatever it will be
You're always there for me

Life In Its Own Way of Seeing It
by Pilar Batista

I've always gotten through the risk of going through my challenges,
But they've never gone far.
I feel overprotected over something that happens, but never came to my head.
I don't feel scared of taking a challenge or a risk
That I know I will get into trouble with, but I don't care.
I feel like a sign that says "for rent" at the front of a house. Then saying "sold."
I shiver into the darkness of my madness.
The warmth it gives me is so extravagant, but it goes and comes back ...
Once in a blue moon.
To some people, this might sound disturbing, but they're wrong.
Everything is not what it seems in my life. No one understands but me.
You never know how and where your life is going to end.
So you've just got to live your life.
Everything will be fine when your feelings are gone.
I'm getting sick of this. I can't be mad or angry; it's just that I'm weak.
I want to cry, but I can't.
I have this anger in my life that I want to hold back, but it won't come out.
It's making my life, and me, stiff. And what is coming out is attitude.
I have such strong emotions.
I'm not scared of lions and tigers and bears, what I'm scared of is ...?
Life isn't so hard. It's hard if you don't take care of it.
I've always wanted someone to answer this question–
Who would I be if I weren't me? And it never got answered correctly.
Do I want to die? No. Do I want to live in this kind of world? No.
Do you know how many times I'm going to say depressed? Hundreds of times.
And that's the only question that someone answered correctly.
Not from one person, but many.
I never really liked the way I felt this way. I feel sober.
You know I never show my feelings to anyone ...
But to the person or people who read this.

A Man
by Kaylee Thackeray

Can you picture a frightened man lying on the street cold as stone
Without a home
As the wind blows right through the holes in his clothes he shivers
A car drives by, looks at this man, keeps driving and laughs
You feel so bad for this man because he has nobody to love or care for
Who will save this man as he lies there
And hopes he might be able to have a decent meal that night?

I Have Cried
by Julia Towne

A hurricane has happened
Everything is lost
I have not cried
My dreams have been snapped
Like a broken flower
I have more fear than ever
I have not cried
I've drifted away from everyone else
And I can't swim back
I have not cried
A hurricane has torn everything apart
My dreams have been broken
Like a flower
I have drifted away from everyone else
I have cried

Sounds
by Sam Burk Schwarzwalder

I don't want to hear
Gunshots at night, sirens whistling
Footsteps running through my alley
I don't want to hear
Sounds of anger, sounds of hate,
Sounds of violence, sounds of rape
The noise of pain is everywhere,
In the water, in the air
I want to hear the sounds of peace
Birds chirping, children playing, people laughing
The sounds of water in a stream, wind in a chime
If only I was deaf to reality

Our Single Celled Friends
by Michael DiCosmo

I hate germs,
Yes, I do
They hurt my tummy and give me the flu
When I'm sick, I scream, "Boo!"
I hate germs, and they hate me, too

Daze
by Jennifer Teneyck

Thirty days hath September, April, June and November
All the rest have thirty-one.
Except February, which has twenty-eight.
All the children count the days until it finish or let it glaze.
Running, running down the street, asking people the day of the week.
Today is the thirty-first then the next day
Will be the twenty-first.
All the day of the week, in the shower I go and weep
Because the days are going back
I pray to God to give them back.

Almost Summer
by Richard Charity

You pass me in the hall and look my way
Then you silently turn away
Only to slowly look back and smile
As I gently lift your day
Our eyes meet again
Once in L.A. and twice in detention
I love giving you my attention
I like to see you here, enjoying your day
In these stuffy classrooms as time ticks away
Slowly but surely, the days go by
And my eyes are drawn to you, my, oh, my
Towards the end of the day comes time to go
and I will sorely miss you so
As spring turns turns to summer
We share one last smile
Because I won't see you for a while

Nighttime Might
by Samantha Mimoso

Early birds annoy me
Why can't they just let me be?
Night owl's the way to go
Sleep all day, stay up all night
We play and scare with all our might
We let the moon light our way
While we stay up and play
Nothing can get in our way
Total darkness calls us near
Everything will be clear
A moonlit night waits for us
The moon shines bright
Even in the night
Sunrise is around the corner
Playtime is over
Let the long wait begin
For the stillness of the night
To bring forth the might
When the dark is here

If You Leave
by Morgan Kelleher

Please don't leave anytime soon.
Everyone says the sky won't fall,
But I think everything will come crashing down.
Everything will seem so empty.
Like you say.
A nose without freckles is like a night without stars.
You're like a living dream that never goes far.
A piano with no melody.
You're like a wish come true.
I just hope the star I wished upon won't fall
Like all of the others.
A heart that feels beatless, a sky that seems restless, will come to me.
So please, don't let it be,
This will happen, if you leave.

Murky Blue Dreams
by Emma Easler

Murky blue dreams
Echo through my brain
As a tear drop falls in pain
Then happiness saves the day
Worry drops like an atom bomb
As my heart throbs
And all of the emotions of my life
Meet in my murky blue dreams

The Flower
by Sabrina Pellunat

The flower is pink and purple
Petals fall off when the wind blows
No one knows where it goes
It flies in the dirt and sand
Which is why we must understand
As time passes by, the season changes

I Am
by Jerry Francois

I am brave and a genius
I wonder about my future
I hear clouds cry
I see lightning
I want to touch the stars
I am brave and a genius
I pretend I am a judge
I feel God's halo
I touch a shooting star
I worry about gangs
I cry for my family
I am brave and a genius
I understand your loneliness
I say, "Accomplish what you start."
I dream of nonviolent days
I try not to cry
I hope the earth stays peaceful and quiet
I am brave and a genius

A Car Ride
by Sabrina Woods

I sit in the car,
Half asleep,
Watching birds fly,
Foxes spy,
The big grassy plains,
Crystal clear waters.
While I sit in the car,
Wishing I could fly,
It all passes me by.

Painful Love
by Raven James

Painful love is not okay,
But painful love will never go away
Stressing and crying is what I say. I say never, not today
When love is painful, you just have to walk away
You are crying all day, not figuring out what next to do or to say
When your heart is broken, it is never what you expected,
It's just a bad token
Painful love will never stay
Just don't let anyone else take your love away

Sports
by Thomas R. Hering, Jr.

Summer time practices
Practice makes perfect
Outstanding sportsmanship
Run and get healthy
Trying your best
Strength is in your body

Video Games
by Adriana Sakatos

Even if I play them every day.
Even if they rot my brain.
I seem to love them.
I never go outside.
I would never go down a slide.
I'm inside rotting my brain.
My eyes are glued to the screen.
I think they're turning green.
If you turn off the T.V. I will scream.
I won't eat or drink.
My fingers have muscles now.
I'm inside rotting my brain.

My Friend's Birthday
by Robert A.C. Martin

It's Abram's birthday
We're all playing laser tag
And eating pizza

Our Corner
by Megan Chaganis

In the late afternoon, when the earth seems to glow,
My eyes weave through the trees and dimmed forest.
My shadowed yard makes me feel safe, at home.
The birds sing through the breeze,
Ruffling the trees shifting the light in the forest.
The elements of nature, the setting so still,
Makes our corner of the earth feel perfect, feel contained.
The thought of the entire world seems so small, so simple.
I look up the clear blue sky,
A dull smudge of the moon slips through the surface.
Wisps of clouds are splashed on to the sea that looks down on our corner …
… And the world doesn't seem so small.

Flames of Disaster
by Bishoy Said

When flames go high
Don't go nearby
When you hear fire trucks
Watch in amazement as they
Put out flaming chunks of
Fire when the fire is low
It is time to go but don't go
To close the inflamed building
Might collapse just hope a fire
Is not at your house fires can
Spread so be careful

I Wish
by Ashley De Leon

I wish for happiness in the universe
I wish I was rich so that I could help my family out
I wish my mother didn't have to work
I wish that every person on the street had a home
I wish I could live forever with my family
I wish homework didn't exist
I wish school was as easy as playing
I wish that all wishes would come true

Falling Into Fall
by Arianna Aquino
The wind blows
The trees don't grow
Birds can't sing
Not yet spring
Leaves flutter
Bells ring
When is summer
I miss its colors
Above everything
Fall is here
And we can't make it disappear
So just enjoy it
You'll endure it
You're just falling into fall

The Exam
by Haley McMullen

My heart thumps as the silence envelopes the room
The only sound is the shuffling of papers and the steady drum of pencils on wood
The clack of heels echoes in the tiny space, too tiny, the walls are closing in
The paper flutters onto my desk, my breath grows louder and longer
The words are jumbled, I can't make sense of it
I should have studied, absorbed more, eaten less ... I'm going to hurl
I take a gulp of air, my vision clears, the answers flood my brain ... I can do this

The Earth
by Louis Farfan

This Earth is our home
To all humans and trees
And the same goes for the animals
The birds, the bears, and the bees.
Now the Earth is a trash can
It's not looking its best.
If we don't start preserving soon,
All of us will be next

Falling
by Preetkaran Saran

Off I went, I climbed and climbed
The sun kissed my face, the soft, green leaves chimed
The blue sky, cloudless and sunny
The ambient spring air, as crisp as fresh money
Then, sudden fear in my spine made my eyes pop
My body rocked back and forth as I fell from the top
Nature shook violently as I cut through the silent spring air
I glared at the tree, which had shrugged me off as it didn't seem to care
The breezy wind felt cool on my falling skin
The air calm enough to hear the dropping of a pin
But I shouldn't
I wouldn't
I definitely couldn't
Because the strangling grasp of fear had overcome me
Everything was a green and brown blur, too fast to see
As I neared the ground, I could almost feel the painful, upcoming bump
My back felt the grass, and I landed with a "Thump!"

3rd Place

Lyndsay Head

Lyndsay is a happy seventh grade student
who enjoys writing and spending time with friends.
The author of "You Are,"
her faith shines through in the talent
with which she has been blessed.

You Are
by Lyndsay Head

You are the One who died for me,
The One who cried for me,
The One who stands up for me in troubled times,
You are my Creator,
You are my Friend,
You hold my world in Your hands,
You are the One whom I worship,
You are my Father,
The One whom I love.

2nd Place

Ashley Huston

Ashley is a straight A student
who is very active at school,
playing violin for the orchestra
and competing on the dance team.
She loves books, music, and especially poetry.

My Love, You Are
by Ashley Huston

The breath of angels dances through the night sky
A single petal stands valiant in the dark:
My love, you are the single petal
The sly fox stares up into bleakness
Blinded by a single spark of light's radiance:
My love, you are that spark
A tear rolls down a widow's face
In memory of lovers lost
My love, you are that tear
Oh, petal who is my greatest joy
Oh, spark that is my heart's beacon through despair
Oh, tear that is an ocean of sorrow
My love is lost, yet remains in my heart

1st Place

Jennifer Coleman

In addition to being a wonderful writer,
Jenny is an excellent student and avid reader.
This busy seventh grade student
swims, plays piano, cooks, does arts and crafts,
and still makes time
to look after her pet parakeet, Tic Tac.

Poseidon
by Jennifer Coleman

Ten thousand years asleep, asleep
Beneath the caverns of the deep,
The monster rears his head again
To take revenge on worlds of men.
With hiss and snarl and firm-set jaw,
The monster bears each tooth and claw
And bounds for surface, sun and sky,
For sails the ship, the Terrified.
He rips the sail and splits the bow,
The horror and the panic grow.
The crew and pilot turn to flee
And pray for mercy from the sea.
They sink to haunt the ocean realms,
The captain standing at the helm.
The waters now at last are still
The evil one has had his fill.
The sky as blue as was before,
Poseidon lies becalmed once more.
Ten thousand years asleep, asleep
Beneath the caverns of the deep.

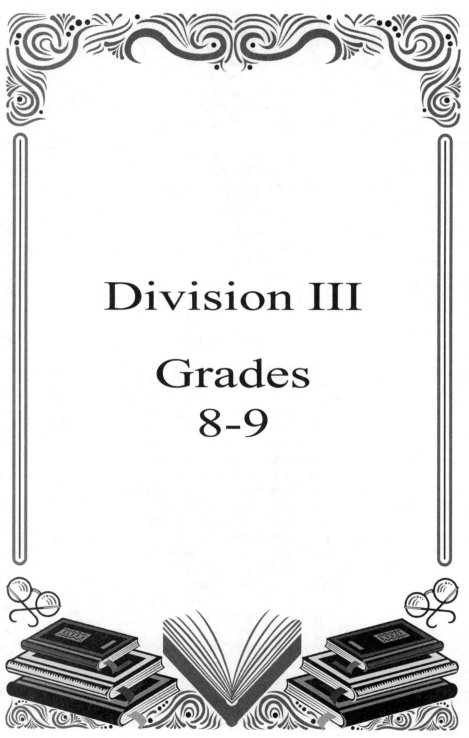

Division III

Grades
8-9

Dancing, Dancing, Dancing
by Dionna Hargrove

Dancing around as quiet,
As can be,
Dancing around I can't
Hear her feet,
Dancing around in Europe
I see,
Dancing around in the
TV screen,
Dancing around now where is
She now,
I don't know she is nowhere
To be found,
I think she is still dancing
In Heaven where the
Angels go.

Gone
by Taylor Mailloux

Sitting here in the dark of night,
Trying not to cry with all my might.
What made you leave without saying goodbye?
I have nothing now, so I just cry,
Tears start falling down my face,
I fall asleep and drift into space.
In my dream I see me and you,
But it's just a dream, as I can see.
I then wake up and start to scream for you.
Now you're gone forever.
There's no bringing you back, never!
There'll just be that hole in my heart,
It will be there as long as we're apart.
But, I just gotta move on,
Just gotta live with the fact you are gone.
Next time please don't say
You'll be there always,
It'll just be a lie,
Makes people die inside.

My Pen
by Dallanara Taveras

This is my pen
I have more, almost ten
But I love this one of all
It's smooth and has a rolling ball
This is my pen
It's one out of ten
Its ink is black and shiny
And it's not all that tiny
This is my pen
I use it when I can
It's really nice and pink
But it's run out of ink

White Pebbled Shore
by Brittany Bursa

The chimes cling together
With the passing winds
The shells rub gently
Taking me back to the beach
The waves crash
Against the white pebbled shore
Seagulls whine
In search of food
As the breeze glides over the surface
A cool chill passes through me
Goose bumps rush over my arm
Serenity present
Mind at ease
I awake from my daydream
To the cool October morning
The chill is unbearable
Yet I stay out for just a minute more
My brain is numb
No thoughts enter or leave
I stand at the edge of my deck
Toes hanging over
Wisps of hair fall onto my face
I brush them off gently
Thinking only happy thoughts
- In loving memory of Thomas J. Callahan

The Sun
by Lee Tallaksen

The sun is like a ball of fire
In the sky, higher and higher.
Lights the sky every day
It is there when we pray.

Indian Lake
by Chloe' Lyden

This lake sings songs to me,
Songs of joy and laughter.
I go there for fun, to play, and socialize.
Everyone there is your friend.
They all hear the lake's song.
Its water is clear as glass.
Once you jump in, it soothes you like an old friend.
The magical lake is full of memories,
And every day you make a new one to always remember.
They all hear the lake's song.

Grandma's Loyal Friend
by Adam Ahmad

My grandma has a sweet companion
He is small and precious too,
He keeps my grandma content
And out of the blue.
Strong as a German Shepard
Who never wanders astray,
He plays and dotes upon Grandma
And brings joy to Grandma's days.
Grandma's dog is a friendly soul
Whimpers and cackles in joy,
Who never frightens my grandma
And is just like a little boy.
Grandma's companion is soft and fluffy
Cuddles with her to sleep,
Extenuates her rough times
With him she cannot bear to weep.
He follows her into the pasture
To pick radiant wild flowers,
His company is light and pure
During life's entire sojourn.

Lonely "N"
by Amanda Sarria

"Pizza at three?"
"Man you know where I'll be."
Yeah, but how about me?
Books, books, and books galore
Ask me not, go ahead and ignore.
Feelings – I have none
It's okay, make fun
You can tease, push, and shove
Make sure you know He's watching over from up above.
You go ahead and play your game
Just be aware that you're causing Him shame
Heaven or Hell, this is your choice.
Speak up now, or have a forever unheard voice.

Courage Is
by Katia Woods

What is courage?
Courage ...
Courage is being brave and fearless.
Courage is like the sun peeking through ominous clouds on a dark day.
Courage is Dr. Martin Luther King, Jr.
The sun feels brave when it defeats thunderous clouds and shares its sunshine.
Courage means shining bright and having a smile even when scared.
A person who remains loyal and honest to his beliefs has true courage.
Courageous children are catalysts for change.
Courage means taking risks and standing up for what one believes in.

Something We Must Accept
by Daniel Satalino

Confused is my state of mind
Thoughts have passed through my head.
Why is there war?
Why do we enjoy watching people die?
Why guns and not words?
Why war and not peace?
Like carnivores feed on meat,
We feed on violence.
It is simply something
We cannot do without

It's Just Not the Same
by Amber Norton

You're my inspiration–well, at least, you were ...
You taught me that you were different from everyone else,
You taught me that I shouldn't care what people think about me.
But, when you left, I was hopeless. I lost my will to do everything.
I'm absolutely nothing without you.
Remember when you told me, "Yeah, don't ever give up,
'Cause my little peanut can do anything. I believe in you, trust me."
Well, I thought I could. But now I'm fourteen years old,
I learned that people come and go just like that. In the blink of an eye.
And guess what? You're one of them.
I thought you could actually be a father. But I guess I was wrong about you, Dad ...
You're just another man, a guy who thinks he can be whatever he would like,
But face reality, Dad; you're absolutely nothing without your daughter by your side.
And you wanted me to be just like you, getting down 'n dirty.
But guess what, Dad? You no longer have your little girl anymore,
She's grown, and she has forgotten you–every little bit and piece of you.

A Chance
by Paramjyot S. Bakshi

Around you, I feel inside out; I get nervous and don't know what to say
I stand there, letting your smile fill my heart
Taking in the sound of your voice, day after day
Love is what my heart was filled with until the day you walked away
I hated myself for falling in love again yet still, I love you more everyday
All you did was walk out of my life, barely saying a goodbye
You just left me in the dark, by myself, all alone, to cry
In my mind, I always see you turn away from me
Thinking of nothing but the thoughts of you just forever leaving me
I don't know what else I can say, or what I should do
All I can think of is that there is nothing for me but to wait for you
All these poems I write will be only to you, from me
I wish for us to be close together again for all eternity
Every time I think of you, I fall into a trance
I picture us dancing together, feeling nothing but love and romance
I love you more than anything and wish for us to forever be, again
But all I ask from you now is for just another chance ...

Love
by Valerie Peter

Love is a land of hopes with no bounds
Love is a land with no noise, no sounds
Love is a gift, a treasure
A life with love is full of pleasure
You can never be sad with love in your heart
Love is something that you can't tear apart
Love is a river that constantly overflows
When you find that special one, it always shows.

Time
by Amber S. Feeney

Time! Where are you going? Come back! Won't you stay?
I'm still maturing, Don't you see?–Every single day?
I'm sorry that I'm still a half of what you wanted me to be,
But I'll need you along the way; please, just hear my plea.
It's been hard to realize what a treasure you could be,
And it's been a while since I thought about you, what you could really mean to me.
I understand that I've never thought twice, you don't deserve this, I know,
But I ask that you would be forgiving once more,
But if you must leave then please leave with peace,
And with just one last goodbye.

Trapped
by Franklyn Vega

In this corner, I stand alone.
Dark and lonely, like Al Capone.
Maybe, one day, I'll leave the shadows,
And go into a lake that's shallow.
Never seen the light of day,
But put into the dark to play.
Hearing the wolves hunt and howl,
I also hear the leader's growl.
Feeling the need, the need to write,
My poems will never be out of sight.
Rats eating me alive,
How ever will I survive?
It's agonizing pain.
I hope I'm still sane.

Red-Curtained Bliss
by Joe Maybloom

The lights of the stage blinding my eyes
I forget who I am and reach for the skies
The character I play becomes my life
I live in their shoes and feel all their strife
The feeling to leave yourself behind
Become someone else for a period of time
The applause from the watchers below your field
Your heart skips a beat, and it is your shield
The tears and the pain are left in the wings
Your mind leaps with joy and your heart sings
The lights of the stage blinding my eyes
I forget who I am and reach for the skies

Black
by Joe Pickard

Black is the darkness inside us, the evil next to our heart.
It's the endless pits, and vast space ...
Coming in various shapes and sizes.
The shadow that stalks you, or death that could be lurking around the corner.
Black is everywhere, and there's no way of hiding from it,
From shirts and pants, to crayons and markers.
It's the smoke of our world, later turned into ashes.
It's like our bruises when we fall off our bikes.
It's the numbers of a speed limit sign, which no one obeys.
Black is when we want to relax; close our eyes; sleep.

You're the Growing Pain
by Anna Krisak

The pain inside is growing like nothing before
All that has happened; the deceit
And you telling me the opposite; lies.
Just makes it all get worse and worse
It hurts, and makes me feel this hate.
I never wanted this to happen,
But I guess it did; explain why.
Remember what we use to be?
It was so much better, right?
The unfortunate thing is that we're finished,
No longer wanting to go back
Or is that only what we said?

Get Me Out
by Sara Danielczyk

I'm sitting here
Everyone is staring.
My face turns ghostly pale
I start to shake.
I look around
Their eyes are piercing through my soul.
My throat turns desert dry
I want to hide.
Chills are traveling down my spine.
My heart dives into my stomach.
I break into a cold sweat.
No one shows concern.
The room turns upside down.
My head has gone blank.
I can't take it anymore
Get me out!

True Love
by Mattie Egerter

You are the apple of my eye,
The hop in my step,
The skip of a heartbeat
When walking by,
The touch of our fingers,
The static of our lips,
The connection of our eyes
When in love.

David
by Julia Vallejo

He's kind and understanding.
He's strong yet sensitive.
He's smart yet so lost.
At times he's harsh and demanding.
With his sensitive and understanding, he's very tentative.
He wastes so much time with anger and can't see the cost.
I wish I could understand him.
I wish I were as strong and sensitive.
I wish I could bring him comfort from his exhaustion.

Last Days
by Jonathan Sanchez

Our days together are coming to an end
No more laughter or fun
The days are getting shorter and shorter by the minute
Something that could never be stopped or changed
The once happy and fun days are now filled with anxiety
As we drift away to our own separate paths
It becomes more difficult to understand we won't be together anymore
This concept can be sometimes hard to understand
Being apart from each other
New horizons will always be open
But our friendships will never die out
Friendships that we cultivated for many years
Won't be broken apart into little pieces
Counting the days before we leave
We think of everything we have done so far
Memories that could never be destroyed
Wander our heads as the last day draws near
The last day is finally here
Bye!

Your Love
by Shauna Randall

Your love means a lot to me.
It reminds me of some honey.
It's very sweet and it clings to me.
I wonder why that might be?
Your love means a lot to me.
Your love is unlike any other.
It's very different from that of a brother.
It's very strange, because it hovers.
And now I know why your love is unlike any other.
Your love is my everything.
It's perfect, because it has no strings.
Your love makes my heart sing.
Your love is my everything.
Your love makes my heart dance.
It runs around and does a little jig.
When you're around, my heart will prance.
Your love makes my heart very big.

Lost Love
by Dugan Walsh

We had our own idea of fun
Love was weaved when each other were together as one
Doing everything imaginable and some
Catching each other's emotions and meanings
Eyes to heart to lungs
She was an artist, sculpting me into whatever she wanted
I followed into what seemed a utopia
She was an actor, curing every pain I ever thought and had
Love was not comfort then, yet a journey for it like a nomad
Glimpse at a higher social hierarchy
She wasn't cool enough for me
Foolishly, we separated like Moses and the sea
Now she moves on to new, young Romeo's
And I am the shadow of her heart and soul
Another chapter of her life unfolds
Disgust to my eyes and ears
The worst way to miss someone is not when they are too far away
But the clear cut opposite
An obscene knife to an easy dream
The worst way to miss someone is when they are right next to you
But you know that it's impossible to ever have them back

The Conquering Force
by Christina Toms

The thick forest, dark as a starless night,
I run through, heart pounding, engulfed in fear.
Dense leaves cast black shadows, blotting out light,
Struggling through the murk, the path is not clear.
A frightened young bird learning how to fly,
About to be thrust into the unknown,
With tentative wing beats, takes to the sky.
In exultance, its crimson plumage shone.
Cracks snake their way through the broken mirror,
Distorting everything in its regard.
As I gaze at the shattered exterior,
The image within is forever marred.
Uncertainty twists and conquers the mind,
Making one's goal even harder to find.

Let Go
by Paolo Sanchez

You mock the truth, yet it is nothing to fear,
The reason you do this–this is uncertain.
The time to reveal is right now and here,
Come out from the dark and nightmarish curtains.
Step aside from the bowels of darkness,
Let these shadows devour you no more.
Come towards the warmth and let be the coldness,
Speak the truth from here and forevermore.
I beg you to let go of your old ways.
As it's time for you to begin new days.

The Real Me
by Brianna Knight

Brianna
Talkative, caring, nice, and happy
Sister of Jasmine,
Lover of hot summers, friends, and cheerleading
Who feels happy when with friends, sad when alone, and scared when in the dark,
Who needs smiles, happiness, and respect,
Who gives care, laughs, and love,
Who fears school, competitions, and bears,
Who would like to see Paris, to become a singer,
And to have our economy problems to get better.
Who lives in a big house in New Jersey.
Knight

Let Go
by Maria Stevens

I try not to care,
But deep inside I do.
Why is it so hard
To let go of you?
I shed a simple tear,
Unwanted and unkind.
Why can't your beautiful face,
Get out of my mind?
Everything reminds me
Of what used to be.
I wonder if you
Have let go of me?

The Definition of Comedy
by Tyler Pullen

A personal display of glee
An attempt to be funny
In the form of a mockery
An odd show of buffoonery
A remark stated wittily
A statement remarked keenly
A wise comeback made quickly
A response said sarcastically
A phrase pronounced laughably
A voice that's simply silly
An insult making fun of thee
A comment said uniquely
A jest made unusually
A joke pantomimed oddly
An anecdote told pleasingly
A tale announced humorously
A great show of irony
A child acting annoyingly
These things define comedy
And comedy defines me

Reaching For the Stars
by Ibukun Olowookere

Reaching for the stars
Fears
They stop you from reaching the stars
Fears of heights; of people's opinions; of disappointments
And of whatever it is that makes you feel small
These fears control you
But when you conquer, then you're in control
How can you reach for the skies when you're afraid to go higher?
How do you reach for the stars if you're always thinking on how to impress others?
You have to reach for the stars for yourself and no one else
How can you reach for the stars if you're afraid of falling?
Falling is one of the best things that can happen to you, if you overcome!
When you fall, just try harder to stay up, because when you conquer your fears
Then, and only then, can you reach for the stars

School
by Pete Farina

Learning, studying
Education
Smart, fun
School

Two Shots
by Daniel Okai

I'm walking down the street with my girl in my arms
We see this boy crying and we ask him what's wrong
He says nothing while tears fall down
Smashing dead in the ground
I try one more time; he pulls out a gun
What am I supposed to do, sit there or run?
I tried to stop him from shooting
But he didn't listen
We hear two shots and now I'm limping
I looked at my girl and she's flipping out
Now what am I supposed to do, sit there and pout?
Pain rushes through my body,
Like a doctor sticking a needle through my vein
The boy rushes home like an idiot
Because he was sitting right in front of it
I tell my girl to call the cops
But before you do that, call my pops
I'm counting down the last seconds of my life
And to think, this was going to be the day I ask Shonte to be my wife.

Summer Break
by Gina Fox

Summertime and cold ice cream,
It all just seems like one big dream.
Sandy shores and foamy waves,
Boats sail around into the bay.
Walking together on the boardwalk,
While holding hands and talking.
It's here today, but then, disappears,
It's like summer break always ends in tears.

The Faith of Love
by Korin Musa

Another love of words
And a cloud of verses
That you see of the past
In another time,
Love intertwined with loving ideas
Running through the air
Like leaves of autumn.
Images they have erased
Smiles that have disappeared,
Memories that are made
Like ashes of a fire
That thought it was extinguished.

Lily's Volcano
by Candace Funsch

Lily stood alone as the day turned to night
Looking up to the sky
Rain clouds now vanished
Enjoying a breathtaking sunset unfold before her
Far beyond it was a dormant volcano ... or was it?
Now fierce, orange lava suddenly spewed down its side
Erupting with beauty in a vibrant mix of red and pink
The earth began to quietly shimmer
Or was it her quivering legs, anticipating what came next?
She couldn't help but look away
Overwhelmed for a moment
Not quite in fear, but in disbelief
Then the shaking stopped just as quickly as it had started
Lily turned back around, to meet her fate
But all she could see
Was her tranquil reflection in the puddle beneath her
As calm, and still as could be
She stood there staring deep into the shallow water
As the sun gently disappeared beneath the mountain
Along with her reflection.

The Unseen
by Nicole Goodwin

Angels watching over you
You are in a haven of love and happiness
Nothing to hurt you
Nothing to erase your pride
You have an angel by your side
Yet unseen from everyone
Heard by no one, felt by the world
You are loved, and you love them
As they come in all shapes and sizes
No flaws, no broken cracks in that porcelain face of yours
An angel you are
- In loving memory of my Uncle Michael

Peaceful Flyer
by Isabelle Nemeh

Peaceful flyer is so free,
Living its life happily.
Twirling around through the air,
It can travel anywhere.
Peaceful flyer, flying high,
Above the clouds and in the sky.
It flies in flocks, and not alone,
Constantly finding another home.
Peaceful flyer, in a tree,
Singing its wonderful melody.
Chirping its sounds all day long,
Never getting tired of its beautiful song.
Peaceful flyer, so petite,
You can barely hear its little tweet.
It's like a feather, very light,
No wonder it can fly to such a great height.
Peaceful flyer, I think of you,
Longing to explore the view.
It must be nice to see those crowds,
While you are flying in the clouds.

Watch What You Wish For ...
by K-Max Mauer

Three on the wall
One knocked down
Two more to fall
Two on the wall
Then knocked down
One more to fall
One more to fall
Why the frown?
Last one, after all

Autumn's Pleasures
by Tess Hamilton

Branches bow and sway,
Sunlight drips like honey between the pines,
The leaves of the tall slender birches quiver in the lilting breeze.
My skin meets the soft brown earth,
Green tentacles of grass tickle my legs as I sink into a welcoming bed of turf.
Quiet noise surrounds me.
Small creatures, that are hardly noticed by the human eye, are my companions.
My heart sings with contentment,
And I sleep ...
Dreaming of the lovely world in which we live.

War Is War
by Susanna Keilig

Up in the front, we lose our fear.
Hide in the trench, for the enemy's near.
Firing it up; death is our goal.
Pile them up in the nearest shell-hole.
Hand grenades, mortars, and snipers too,
Don't bother us, only recruits who are new.
Go hand to hand; stab in the back,
Pull the trigger; hear the gun crack.
Better keep up, make sure to keep score.
All the fairness in saying that war is war.

The Surprise Snowfall
by Oliver Josephson

It falls on the frosted, dried out ground
From the dark, cloudy sky.
I see huge white snowflakes flurrying through the crisp air,
Blowing down furiously,
Flowing through the towering trees,
Covering the ground; the green grass is a distant memory.
Animals are buried inches under the ground, hibernating.
I am gleeful and free through the falling snow.
There is nothing more exhilarating than a surprise snowfall.

Mourn
by Kayla Lafi

The sun rises,
But my heart mourns.
Your body is wrapped in vines.
I tried to save you and my hands are pricked by the thorns.
The wind blows
Time goes on.
I will go when the rivers stop to flow.
Until then, my love,
The birds will fly above,
The sun will shine,
The wind will blow,
Rivers will flow;
And, therefore, my heart will always mourn

Summer
by Syam Lafi

I love summer.
When it ends, it is a bummer.
My name is Syam.
I like sports in the summer.
I wish I had a Hummer for the summer.
I enjoy football in the summer with my friends.
We all have a good time, until summer ends.
I was born in the summer, and so are some people I know.
I like to have fun with them until it is dark, and I have to go.
This is my summer, which I enjoy, and have fun with many girls and boys.

Lullaby
by Majesta Pruszinski

"L" is for all the little boys and girls who have to live in this freak show of a world
"U" describes the you, who left me in my lonely life
The double "L" means the pure insanity called "life,"
That you can't live with or without
"A" stands for just another person gone from this world
And their memories float away in the wind
"B" is for best friends and back-stabbers, counting as one
"Y" may be in faith and their lullaby

War
by Nicholas Liebhauser

We storm into Iraq like a parade
We're carrying guns and grenades
We hear the captain shout and yell
I open the barrel and insert the shells
I hear the bullets blow past my ear
They are going so fast I can hardly hear
I jump behind a big boulder
I feel a sharp pain in my shoulder
I hear the blood drop to the ground
I see my friend coming from behind a mound
I drop to my knees and look at the sky,
And I ask myself, "Am I going to die?"

The Song (After Mary Oliver)
by Klara Blazek

The first song I ever wrote
Would not stop flowing from my fingertips
And rang out in the quiet amazement of the air
And ended in the slow chords of C minor
Later I opened my book
And separated note from note and wrote them.
Now the music is in me; we are risen, tangled together,
Certain to fade back to silence.
Out of anger, and anger, and more anger
We feed this feverish melody,
We are nourished by the harmony.

Shyness
by Andrew Daniels

Standing in front of the room, all eyes on me,
I hate being shy like this
Why can't I be like a rock star,
Bouncing and booming off the walls?
I wish I was like that, but, no,
I say a wrong word, I stutter,
My face blows up with heat,
My whole body shakes like an out of control car.
I look like a wavering fish, out of water
Just think, if I could; cool down someway,
People laughing at me; got to do something.
My best bet is to laugh along,
Have fun for the two minutes I speak,
Even if I do mess up ...
Oh well, it is just another day in school

Tutti-Frutti
by Allen Fernandez

Birds chirping outside
Me inside, eating noodles
Chickens outside, too
Me watching TV
Playing with my broken shoe
Just one day at home

I Believe
by Daija Baptist

I believe that my dreams will come true
Even now, or from when I was two
I believe I can, and I believe I will
Eventually see that all of my dreams are real
I believe that, someday, you and me
Can look at the stars and set our dreams free
I believe that my dreams can show reality
And it helps me show my personality
I believe that my prayers are heard and loved
By God and by all the above
I believe, if you try, you will succeed
In your hopes, prayers, goals, and dreams

Encaged
by Anjani Shah

Sometimes I feel like this is a game I lost.
I feel as if I've paid the ultimate cost.
Shattered dreams find their home
But still alone, they cannot roam.
Encaged in bars of solitude,
They've been treated nothing less than crude.
Try to find an escape route,
You face the world with arms spread out.
Through the rain and ice,
Promises have been enticed.
I struggle through the black air,
But these memories are not repaired.
And as I've watched the grass grow,
I see the love you have sowed.
My brain is the target of all these mistakes.
And so I try, to step on these brakes.
They've tried to find me in this dark but dreary light.
But there is more to see than this internal fight.
There's something to see behind my brown eyes.
There's more to my life than a sad goodbye.

Tunnel of Life
by Alexandros I. Kalos

Sky so blue, grass so green, this seems so perfect.
As I walk this road, the sins come back, slowly to haunt me.
The blue sky becomes engulfed in dark grey,
And the green grass becomes an unfriendly black as I slowly progress forward.
Soon, the light disappears, and the black swallows me.
The darkness laughs, and the dampness surrounds me.
The sorrow and paint echoes throughout,
The darkness a thousand voices calling out for help.
I try to pretend it's not there, try to ignore it, but it's there and I know it.
I begin to run, try to escape, the darkness follows.
What has become of me?
If only I could turn back and avoid this path.
But as I run, I see light at the end of this. Redemption.
As the end grows near, the light grows too, and soon it embraces me.
As I rejoice, I remind myself to change my ways.
And so I take a new path, a new man.
The sky so blue, grass so green.

Global Warming
by Brenda Perez

It used to be a prediction, but now it is a reality.
They thought the Earth was made of metal,
They thought we did not have to worry about it.
The North and South Poles are melting like ice cream on a sunny day.
They are cutting the trees as if they are sweeping the floor.
They throw trash on the floor like it is their duty.
When I think about this, my head is a volcanic eruption.
Where is Santa Claus going to live?
When I talk about this, my mouth is made of ice.
How are we going to fix this?
When I look at this, my tears are raindrops an a rainy day.
What is going to happen to us?
We have to do something quick, like a cheetah after its prey.
We are the hungry cheetahs; our goal is our prey.
But don't worry about it,
We still have time, the clock hasn't reach 12 o'clock.
But it's going to, so let's do something really fast.
Before the ticking bomb explodes.
Do you what I'm talking about?
It's global warming; take that as a warning.

Distraction
by Anthony Sclafani

Distraction takes you away from the important things in life,
To make you pay attention to silly things, like sugar and spice
Distraction is a friend who urges you to play all day,
And do nothing else but lay in a field of hay
Distraction lets you ignore your homework and responsibilities,
It helps you forget work and put on your skis
That you will wear without a care,
Nor second thought, or second pair,
For distraction helps you only focus on things in life
That are silly things, like flying a big red kite
Distraction will lead you down a path
That you will never come out of without a scratch
A lot of times, this path never ends
Some people follow Distraction till they decide they've lost their way
I'm sorry, but I cannot finish this poem,
Distraction just came into my room, wanting to play

The Nightmare
by Jessica Ibias

The sun was shinning,
Night in the sky
Shinning on so bright and true
Its heat, its warmth
It feels so good on my skin
The birds were singing,
Singing all around me and the animals.
They were all frolicking about.
Everything looked so peaceful,
But then, things started to change.
Darkness fell, and everything turned deathly quiet.
There was no moon, no stars, nothing
The darkness enveloped me,
And I couldn't breath; I was dying.
But then something happened: I woke up.
It was just a dream, a nightmare.

Where Has the Peace Been Hiding?
by Alexa Pelletier

Race and religion; politics and ideas,
Where has the peace been hiding?
Misplaced from America to Korea,
Segregation is done, time to quit dividing.
Thanks to Martin Luther King and Rosa Parks,
Who helped us achieve this goal.
Standing up for what is right has left everlasting marks,
America should now be in peace as a whole.
But fighting and arguments have caused wars and hate,
Leaving America shattered and broken.
Time to reunite, not start a fight; get peace before it's too late,
Before the final voice has spoken.
"It isn't enough to talk about peace, one must believe it,"
Something that Eleanor Roosevelt once exclaimed,
An idea that so many people do not achieve, you have to admit.
With all the work put into peace, so many people who help could be named.
Paul McCartney, Jimi Hendrix, and John Lennon too,
Fighting for peace and trying to make important resolutions.
Songs, speeches, and literature; all with reasons we need peace to go through,
Peace can happen, all we need is contributions.

Two Wolves In a Forest
by Stephanie Vargas

Two wolves sit side by side in a forest unknown
With wicked old bending trees ...
Of which owls perched on perfectly
In the dead of night, whoo-ting and whoo-ting till they fall asleep.
These two wolves travel, only together, and never alone
These forests are endless
Or so at least they seem ...
Two wolves sit side by side, alone in the dark scary forest
The male wolf cares for the one sitting beside him
No matter what.
They need each other to live, to breathe,
To survive
The forest is no joke to the weak;
So together they are thankful they're both so strong and caring.
Two wolves sit side by side in the forest unknown
Together they stand, together they live, together they breathe
Two gorgeous white wolves
Forever and ever

Step Who?
by Floyd Clark

Why don't you like me? It seems like you love everyone else.
You start stupid arguments for no apparent reason.
Is it because you don't like my mother?
You would always tell me how much I look like her, then put on a wrenched smile.
You take your anger out on me, don't you?
You knew that my mother and father had something special,
But you couldn't grasp that.
It seems like my father was just there to aid you in your time of need.
I wish that I wasn't afraid of you, but I was only five when you stomped into my life.
I remember when I told my mother
That you and my dad where fighting like Power Rangers,
And Dad would always block, while you kept attacking.
He knew not to fight back, no matter how much damage you would cause.
The doctors said that my father's death was stress-related,
And now I know that you were the stress.
You killed one of the most important people in my life,
And I will never forgive you for that.
Some people still ask, "How's your stepmother doing?"
And I reply, "Step-who?

When Night Turns To Day
by Lauren Anzevino

Sunset seeks into darkness,
And the whole world seems to be on mute.
Not a sound
You stop and listen.
That's the only thing you can do.
Darkness surrounds you and the darker it gets, the quieter it gets.
Earth is on pause for a few moments of your life.
The wind is whistling softly and now that's the only thing seen,
Felt or known to be existing.
Darkness is closing in on you,
Drowning you in its lonely, ambiguous mind.
The answer to what you've been seeking is hidden within the whispering wind.
It picks up speed, knocking you off your feet and sweeping you away.
Once thrown to the ground upon the dark pavement of a deserted lot,
Ache and fear creeps through your body,
Seeping through the wounds and bruises.
Looking up at the sky, night is slowly turning to day with the sun beginning to rise
As it always does.
The world seemed to come back to life ... but did it actually?
Will the sun always shine above you? Or one day will the wind take over?

Love
by Nicolle Jaramillo

Roses are red,
Violets are blue,
I'm in love with you.
Why can't you just see it,
I only want you.
These past days without you,
Was so hard,
I don't think I can live without you.
You're my man no one else,
I hope you know that your the first.
Sad that your gone,
Want you back.
Waiting for you everyday,
Day and night.

The Cycle of Life
by Nicole Archibald

One seed
Buried underneath soil
Drenched with water
Baked by Earth's sun
Sprouting out of its comfort zone
Beginning to appear like everyone else–
A stem; leaves; petals
Now pulled.
Brought into new surroundings
Shaken up by the new environment–
A vase
Condensed, like a can of sardines
Nowhere to go, nowhere to be
Gone

The Many Colors of Life
by Megan Wilkens

Green is to live,
Blue is to despair,
Red is to love,
And purple is to hope.
These are all the colors, and everything we need to live.
Without yellow, there is no need to want, no need to please.
We need these colors of life.
With green, we can all live, even when we die.
When we die, we can still live a thousand times over with green.
With blue, we can feel sad, lonely, or dejected.
Blue is the color of dying, but also of new lives being made,
Without blue, there is no life.
To have red is to have compassion, partnership, and family.
Without red, we can't even know happiness, we can't know fun.
But, with red, we'll have just about everything.
Purple is for smiles, laughter, parties, and fun.
If we don't have purple, we don't have weddings, or birthdays.
We only have funerals and death.
But today, and every other day, we will have green, blue, red, and purple.
With those colors, we will have life ...
Life ...
Life ...
Life

Defend
by Athena Bogdanos

I will fight for the rights of everyone here.
I will fight without shedding a single tear.
I will fight while others cower in fear.
I will fight until my path is clear.
This is a fight in which I won't surrender.
A fight in which I'm the eternal defender.
I will defend every age, race and gender,
Until all of the hatred is returned to its sender.
I have made a new resolution.
I will not stop till I get retribution.
This revenge is my new institution.
These are all the effects of my heart's pollution.
I embrace the pain in a whole new light.
I finally grow strong, and finish the fight.
The enemies have lost and gained a whole new sight.
I have finally made everything right.

Alone
by Julia Chavarry

I feel so misplaced and confused,
Tears begin to crowd into my eyes, yet I have no notion as to why.
"What's wrong?" they ask me,
I leap back from my nightmare and smile,
"Nothing, I'm just ... tired."
They wonder what my problem is when I put on a fake smile.
Yet, can any of them possibly comprehend how I suffer?
Why I'm so lonely and shattered?
Constant questions make my head throb and my forehead crease with concern
What will I do?
Is all this just a search for attention and compassion,
Or is this pain for real?
Why can I help no one, and why can no one save me?
Will it ever stop?
Again they ask, "What's wrong?"
But I don't know. I just want someone to rescue me,
But no one understands, and no one knows how.
I am alone.

Jail
by Erika Arana

I feel trapped
It's like I'm in jail
And I can't get out
I'm stuck behind these metal bars
I can't find a way out of this place called life
Everyday I scream, "Help me!"
But no one ever saves me
I am finally free, after fourteen years
I didn't know it was going to be so easy
All I did was believe in myself
And have confidence in myself
I now know who I am
I can finally live my life–and so can you!
Don't be stuck in "jail" for such a long time, like me

One Wish
by Danielle Allgor

If I only had one wish to make,
I'd use it up on you.
Just to see you one more time,
In the Heavenly sky so blue.
But all I have are the memories,
The good ones and the bad.
Just to say I love you,
Would be the best wish I ever had.

The Costume
by Jack Pontrelli

This coming Saturday is Halloween
I'm thinking of something new
It won't be green or hairy scary
And I won't be saying "Boo!"
My costume is hilarious
I really think it's good
My dad thinks it's ingenious
My mom doesn't think I should
My costume screams and drools,
Bites and gives me blisters.
I think of them as monsters
This costume is my sister's.

Pain
by Christian Blomquist

Pain! I feel pain everywhere,
My head, my lungs, my arms, my legs, my stomach, my eyes, my mouth ...
Everywhere my love had touched me ... before she left me here alone
With no help or love in this world of confusion.
My heart has no pain ... all it has is a strange numbing sensation
Like it was poisoned, or tricked, or beaten with a baseball bat and left to die.
All I think of is her!
Everything I look at brings back another
Loving, caring, sad, painful, happy, memory.
It drives me insane.
I feel like my compassion was devoured by a hawk and regurgitated back up.
All I want in this world of hate ... is love from my girl.
But I can't have ... what does not exist!

Addiction
by Sahi Hari

And now the flames are kissing her arms
Burn after burn, charring her skin and numbing her soul
Reflecting in her eyes, turning them a fiery green
Back and forth, pulling her hand across the flame
Feeling it slowly caress her skin
Gently, she dips her finger into the liquid wax
Feeling the scorching coolness against her pale fingertips
Now that every inch of her has been seared and singed
She turns her back on her incandescent addiction

Happiness
by Dylan Hackett

You are the hope in our souls
You are the faith that comes with high goals.
When nothing in our lives seems right,
You remove the night and replace it with light.
When we are blue, that's your cue
To fill us with that warm feeling,
That emotional healing,
Called happiness.

My Shooting Star
by Corinne Cronheim

I just can't forget you,
I regret how much I miss you,
But I don't regret I met you...
Hold my hand and I'll never let go.
You make the move and I'll kiss you.
We'll walk together to the moon,
Staring into each others eyes.
Skipping in the moonlight; laughing.
Thinking about nothing else but each other.
Make a wish, blow out the candles.
Yes, I'll be your star at night, will you be my gleaming light?
All the time I look at you, I know you sneak peeks at me too.
Do you love me like I love you?
I'll walk with you to the moon,
And when I look into your eyes, I sore across the open sky.
Wind blowing through our hair,
You are looking back at me, me looking back at you.
Wow, what a beautiful sight.
Wonderful is right.

Love
by Christine Beylerian

Love is like peanut butter and jelly,
Put in a bag far away.
Hiding in the locker all locked up
Is the love that people are scared to show.
Love only comes out when the time is right.
The right time isn't often.
Love is patiently waiting deep in the heart.
It's waiting for the right key to fit the lock.
Love is all around you, but you don't know it,
Unless it comes out and takes a step.
Love can be sitting on a bench
Or sometimes trying to say something,
On February 14th,
Whether it's big or small,
Love is trying to say,
"This is the right time,
Go ahead, and be my valentine."

The Rain's Music
by Mayra Diaz

The rain pounds on my window, with the pitter-patter of the water,
I am reminded of a piano, being played at staccato.
The thunder rolls on the clouds, like ocean waves at the beach.
It sounds like drums, being beaten by sticks, ever so rhythmically.
As the lightning strikes the ground,
I remember a metronome, that ticks steadily.
When it all comes together, it sounds like a symphony, a chorus of angels.
How marvelous the rain is, how beautifully, it makes music.

Sick
by Francine Vaccari

Sick is a child, a child tired
Tired of being hurt, hurt by others
Sick is a state, a state of being
Being cold, worn, worn by others
Sick of being, being let down
Sick of waiting, waiting for something,
That is not going to come
Sick to a point
A point where it hurts
Sick.

Love-Locked World
by Allison Miller

I keep my hands warm by the beat of his heart,
For it is the only thing that keeps my blood from running cold.
I trip over life's obstacles,
He helps me stand steady,
And makes sure I'm ready for life.
I whisper sweet nothings into his ear,
His blond hair kisses my nose,
I apply the favor.
His love is the oxygen of my life.
His voice is the song of my soul.
Interlocked hands, warmer than hot coal.
He has me intertwined in this emotion, love-locked world
That I am stuck in,
The one thing he can't pull me out of.

The Earth Is Smoking
by Tanvi Parmar

The Earth is like everyone's child,
We have to make sure its health doesn't go wild,
We have to make sure that it doesn't keep smoking,
'Cause dangerous problems we could be provoking,
With every puff of smoke from a car,
We choke the Earth's lungs with toxic tar,
If only one country strives to go green,
It will not be as powerful if, instead, we worked as a global team,
Yes, smoking is an addiction,
But listen to the concerned scientist's predictions,
The same planet that supports our life,
Can also cut our lives like a knife,
What kind of earth would future generations know?
What kind of earth will our grand kids see from their window?
No more rolling, green grass,
But, instead, clouds of poisonous gas,
No more spacious blue skies,
All beautiful creatures of nature would have died,
Is that the kind of earth we want to give to other generations?
Where all of our pollution has committed eternal sins?

9:08
by Delphia Nimene

She wraps her immaculate colored vintage pearls around her neck
Pats her snow white cheeks with the pinkest blush
Putting just enough; not too little, not too much
Pulls up her sunshine yellow cardigan
And zips up her floral ruffled skirt
Slipping her flawless feet into her golden flats,
She walks down the stairs silently as her hips dance around with the ruffles
Now, she sits and waits
Hours go by but he promised to come at 8
The dinner is getting cold and the candle light dims as her sanity starts to fade
At exactly 9:08; no second less, no second more
She opens the curtains and sees him with another
She stares in amazement, traumatized for the moment
9:09, she pulls the curtain closed
Crying out like no other
All that love built up for five years straight,
Just vanished that Spring evening at 9:08

Midnight Wind
by Rachel Schilling

In black the midnight wind quietly blows
When I fall into a wondrous dream
As my butterfly eyelids flutter close
Softly, slowly, the beauty all but gleams
When I fall into a wondrous dream
I have no idea where my mind may go
Softly, slowly the beauty all but gleams
At the heavenly places I don't know
I have no idea where I may go
To escape the horrid reality
At the heavenly places I don't know
I find comfort I never thought could be
The night sky starts to be filled with starlight
As my butterfly eyelids flutter close
I wonder where I will escape tonight
In black the midnight wind quietly blows

Why Shall We Wait?
by Ivana Mitic

Our earth is decaying in the palm of our hands.
There still is hope to save it
Why shall we wait?
The Earth is drowning in our filth.
Let's make this refinement already!
Why shall we wait?
Let's revive this earth; it is our only home.
We need to make this change right now,
Why shall we wait?
Let's not leave it to perish,
Let's rekindle this home of ours.
I know we can make this change,
So, really, why are we waiting?

Darkness
by Silvia Gunderson

Darkness is closing in around me.
I don't feel afraid.
Darkness is my friend.
It comes and keeps me company.
Beyond the darkness, I see
Light patches of flowers.
Colors.
They burn my eyes
And so I return my gaze to the comfortable view of nothing.
Darkness closes in on me completely.

The Small Pumpkin
by Tristen Morrison

I once saw a pumpkin not fit for a fly.
It was no smaller than the center of my eye.
But the fly was hungry it was going to die.
But the pumpkin was already baked into a pie.
For an ant that couldn't even fly.

Flying High
by April Gentles

Gliding around the ring with the wind whistling all around
Hooves pounding on the ground, like drumsticks beating hard on drums
My heart is racing as if it's about to explode
I see the dirt kick up behind me as a big, dark cloud continuing to chase me
But I continue to look straight ahead
All I hear is the breathing of the horse
That blocks out the claps and cheers of the crowd, for this is a crucial point
Five strides before it's time to jump
One, two, three, tightening the reins
Then finally, four, and five, for I am flying again!
Lifting out of my saddle, gripping tightly with my legs, my stomach has dropped
There is a pause in time, waiting for the landing; this is the acme of my jump
First, the front hooves come down, then the back
The jump is completed, and I know I put my whole heart into it
Finally, I can relax and shout victory!

Why?
by Wilmer A. Cedeno, Jr.

Why is the Earth here?
Why are the planets and stars
Here? Why are we here?

Fire Storm
by Dante Sawyer

There is a fiery furnace
That's burning inside of me.
The grazing fire, is blazing red across my heart.
At times, I feel an adrenaline rush,
A rush that can't be stopped.
It makes me want to jump up and down,
Or else I'll feel untouched.
Sometimes, I feel like the sun's core,
And I cannot cool it down.
Even when it's below freezing,
I never want to tone it down.
Sometimes, I see this person,
And I don't know what to do.
So I calm down and feel my internal rhythm,
Before the fire storms!

Love Is...
by Krystal Palummeri

Love is budding
Love is strong, love is bonding
Love is strange, love is deranged
Love is helpful, love is funny
Love is in a woman, love is in a man
Love is hardship, love is frightening
Love is fighting, love is breaking
Love is commitment, love is wonderful
Love is challenging, love is lasting
But I fear that, sometimes, love is brazen

To Me
by Tess Reynolds

He may not be a knight,
And he may not be a king.
He may not be "Prince Charming"
With a gold engagement ring.
He may not be the stars,
And he may not be the moon.
He may not be the ocean,
Or a vibrant blue lagoon.
He may not be the sky,
And he may not be the sea,
But in this cold, loveless world,
He means everything to me.

Sunset On the Beach
by Ariarna Odom

I stand here gazing
I see the bright colors of the sun
Mixing, intertwining
It's mesmerizing
The sun steadily setting
Joining the ocean on the horizon
Slowly melting away
Like a snow cone on a summer's day.

Open
by Anthony Guerriero

Before me, in the open mountains, lay a canyon.
A vast canyon filled with forestation.
Beneath it, lay a serene pond.
An exorbitant pond.
A pond that is as delicate as a porcelain kettle,
I scale the canyon walls, then ... jump,
Plunging into the angry, flowing water.
Then tranquilly swim ashore, to my kayak.
I spot a school of fish, beautiful, vibrant fish,
As if they were a rainbow themselves.
Then, "Sccccccccccc,"
I am immediately propelled under water
By the colossal waterfall,
That seems to touch the sky.

I Can't Feel the Pain Anymore
by Alyssa Gonzales

I can't feel the pain, I can't feel the hurt
Again and again, puncturing through my heart
Getting used to the scars, getting used to the cuts
When will it be over?
Looking down, never up
Making friends with my feet
All alone, by myself
Breaking down on the ground,
Dropping on my knees
Head tilted to the floor
Having everyone to please
Tears overflow
Screaming for help
Not being able to breathe
Not a sound has been made
Being pulled down
Dying alone
Peacefully, quietly, happily
It has all just begun

Me
by Molly Resto

"Who am I?" you ask. I say
"That answer can't be answered in one simple way."
If you asked me to dance, I might do a jig,
I do prefer English to Geometry and Trig.
When it comes to a sport, my favorite is lacrosse,
When I watch softball, my attention is a loss.
I prefer one board instead of two skis,
I like to do rails, and glide through the trees.
I don't like the ocean, I prefer the mountains and the lake,
Because it is easier to water-ski in and out of the wake.
When it comes to fashion, it just plain hurts,
I prefer sweat pants to cute little skirts.
I drink water by the gallon, eat fruit from the vine,
You won't catch me with soda, not anytime.
I prefer the Yanks over the Sox; Giants over the Jets,
My least favorite team is the New York Mets.
When it comes to first cousins, the number's not small,
When you add us all up, there are twenty in all.
I've shared with you what's special about little old me,
And when you look at Molly, you get what you see.

Once Upon a Love
by Kristina Samulewski

December 1st is when I fell in love with you; the sky was a clear blue.
I walked up to you, wrapped in my sweater,
I knew that day everything was going to be better.
I remember the sparkle in your eye as you sang me your favorite lullaby.
"I wrote this song for you," and I knew that those words were true.
That day, hot chocolate had never tasted better;
I can still smell your scent on every love letter.
"Always and forever," that's what you said, until you ripped my heart into shreds.
Each time I was with you, my heart raced, and I just knew
That that had been the reason I was alive,
Because you're the one that kept my blood pumping, to help me survive.
But now that you're gone, I'm up way past dawn.
Thinking of what had happened, the reason why you left me abandoned.
I sit by myself, in a room that was once filled with your voice;
I can only sit here, with no other choice,
And thinking, if I had known it would hurt this much,
I wouldn't need to feel your touch.
I can't seem to face another chapter in my life,
Knowing that I had once dreamed of being your wife.
I now walk down the streets we once raced down,
Thinking each day, I must leave this town.
But, without you, it hurts in every way,
And now, it seems, that on December 1st, the skies will always be grey.

Like No Other
by Bianca Sorto

The day was bright and as silent as a mouse.
I tried to hide all the pain that was bottled up inside me.
I thought today would be like no other.
But, instead, it was like every other day;
Noisy like a garbage truck,
Sad like a rainy day,
And depressing like a funeral.
Of course, the old man is screaming at me,
All I wonder is how does it feel to be loved?
Then I realized I am loved in many different ways;
People love me because I am funny.
People love me because I am caring
But I know there's someone out there that loves me for me.
That is the reason I still have hope that one day will be like no other.
- Dedicated to people out there that hope and wish there will be a better day.

Destruction
by Gabriel Even-Chen

There they wait
Standing tall
Not ashamed of what they are
Soon the lumberjacks will be there
Swinging their axes
Chopping down the trees that are so meaningless to them
But still, they stand tall
They are chopped
Twig by twig
Branch by branch
Until they are nothing more than a pile of logs

Skiing
by Griffin Yianakopolos

Swiftly
Knifing through the snow
Intense rush as we
Immerse ourselves in the thrill
Never stopping
Gone

The Poem About Poems
by Chris Beischer

Poems are super-duper cool
You can write them anywhere, even school
I once wrote a poem, while in a pool
Poems can be about anything, maybe even a stool
A poem is special, it is the mind's learning tool
And after you read this, please don't think I am a fool!

An Inconsiderate Child
by Robert Bahmer

I state at the TV screen,
Enthralled, as people are destroyed,
By machine guns and bombs.
A shot from an enemy tank
Blows a soldier to pieces,
And I laugh,
Entertained by the deaths of millions
Years later I lie, in the mud.
Surrounded by screams,
Of pain and death
I stare at the bullet hole,
Opening a gateway into my chest,
And I understand.

Behind My Soul
by Monika Michaluk

Broken deep inside
Thousands of pieces behind my soul
Too hard to clean them up
Feels like I'm inside an empty dark hole
Empty dark hole
Deep inside my chest
Never to be gone
And never will I rest
All the dark memories
All smashed hiding in the hole
It will never be gone
For it is buried deep behind my soul
The pieces behind my soul
Hunt every night
Leaving me with nothing more
But deep, horrifying fright

Beauty
by Sara Markowitz

Tangled hair dried
From the desert air
As the merciless sun beats down
Igniting fire in her
Dull black eyes.
Skin brown and weathered
Worn and wrinkled
As her calloused feet
Keep pace to the drum.
Scars on her hands
And the blue veins stick out
As she raises them above her head
And sways them, like a snake.
Her eyes close at last
And her cracked lips turn up
And open, as she sings.
Time stands still, the desert chills
As it trembles
To her voice.

Window
by Ashley Valenti

I am clear but you can also see right through me.
You can see everything that exists outside.
Whether it's the birds chirping, the trees swaying back and forth,
The wind blowing through the grass,
Or the children playing ball outside.
Whether it's the lightning bolts bouncing off the cement,
The thunder howling in the night time sky,
The clouds swirling around and around in circle,
Or the deadly hurricanes taking away
Several innocent lives.

First Christmas
by Jade McLaughlin

On the colorful television screen,
A small girl is sitting on a tired looking beige couch
She has a cute, ruffled, green dress on,
A glittery, shimmering gold bow in her deep brown hair, a wide smile on her face,
And twinkling brown eyes, reflecting the bright, multi-colored lights
On the colorful television screen,
The date is December 25, 1995
Many tall grownups are crowding around the small, bewildered girl
Watching, waiting for something
On the colorful television screen,
A youthful, petite Asian woman with short black hair hands the small girl a box
It is wrapped perfectly, with shiny silver paper
The woman rips a rough tab of the shiny paper off, and hands the tab to the girl
The small girl pulls the tab, and more,
And thrashes her chubby arms up and down
Having the time of her life
Sitting on the worn out beige couch,
I stare into the eyes of the small girl and remember the time,
13 years, 3 months, and 17 days ago,
When everything was a miracle

Love
by Corey Ginn

Love is like the red and orange sunset
Where the water and the skies met
Love is like a couple gazing in each others eyes
Smooth and long like when cupid arrow flies
Love is like a flower that blooms in the spring
Slow and beautiful as the blue birds sing
Love is destiny, a connection between two, or fate
But to be loved it's a risk you have to take

Becoming An American
by David Chong

I've come to adopt this country
As my own,
I hope to pledge my
Allegiance to the U.S.
And by
Serving this wonderful nation,
As an officer in the military,
I will feel like I am
Giving back what She gave me—
An education, friends, a place,
To call home
The debt
I can not ever repay,
But nevertheless,
I will try

Once More
by Judith Zhang

To set foot in the forest once more, my lasting wish
To hear the crackling of leaves underfoot,
To see the rows of trees all jumbled together like a maze.
To roam freely among the plants and along the towering trees.
Yes, to set foot in the forest once more, my only wish.
To set foot in the forest once more, my lasting wish
To get a glimpse of the animals' domain.
To hear the birds' lilting song,
To see them drink as the water rushes quickly past.
Yes, to set foot in the forest once more, my only wish.
To set foot in the forest once more, my lasting wish
To feel the gentle breeze, and
To hear the soft rustling of the leaves,
To breathe in its natural yet rich air.
Yes, to set foot in the forest once more, my only wish.
Only be swift, for my dying breath is nearing.
Yes, to set foot in the forest once more, my only wish.

3rd
Place

Haleigh Swansen

Talented is an understatement when describing Haleigh.
In addition to now being a published author,
she is also a singer, dancer, and musician.
Her faith is her most prized possession,
and she is often found volunteering
with the youth at her local church.

The Artist
by Haleigh Swansen

I sit in awe behind the Artist, clad in a greasy smock,
Peering over His great shoulder for a glimpse of His easel
My eyes flit hungrily from tip to base of each stolid, ominous mountain
And when they finally lock on the river slicing through the valley,
I'm speechless.
I want to plunge into the foamy froth, laugh with it, dance with it.
I have to force my eyes away,
And when they reach the blank canvas at the top,
My brow furrowing in confusion,
The Artist laughs, as if He knows what I'm thinking.
The bristles of His brush kiss the emptiness, flooding it with majestic sunset.
Then He cranes His neck to see My canvas.
I rush to hide it, but I know He's already seen
The barrenness, the lack of brilliance, the wasted paper
And I, His student, am ashamed.
He smiles, so patient, so understanding,
Places the brush between my fingers,
And wraps His giant, warm hand around my clammy one
"Don't be afraid," He coaxes, so gentle, so kind, "I'll show you how"
And we paint a masterpiece
Together.

2nd Place

Sarah Stratton

It's no surprise, given the quality of her work,
that Sarah loves to write, especially about horses.
In fact, she spent two years on staff at her school's literary magazine.
She also enjoys soccer and horseback riding,
and one day hopes to become a veterinarian.

The Tempest
by Sarah Stratton

Behold, the storm-tossed tempest
Waves, the seaweed manes
Of foaming horses
That race with thunder at their heels
The flash of lightning
Caught in the glare of a fiery eye
With spray spewing forth from their nostrils
Poseidon's herd leads the charge
To clash against the rocky shore

1st Place

Jarred Worley

This ninth grade student admits
he is obsessed with the arts,
dividing his time between
writing poetry, painting, and music composition.
His creative genius is apparent
in the following award-winning piece.
Congratulations, Jarred!

On a Peppermint In a Hotel Room
by Jarred Worley

Crushed red candy of the ancient guild of delight.
Crawls after being stomped on and gathers hair and dust.
The sticky lips and stripes scream of the non-concentric irregularities.
The shards of guarding the hissing words of slander
Have been cracked and shattered, the mirror of innocence,
The pinwheel of childish demeanor!
Now, the tongue of the vacant vagrant walks out and lolls,
Dipping and dripping the saliva out in streaks and pools of distrust.
The casting off of an old life with the crunch of a past regret
And the residue of grief on the black heel of a shoe.

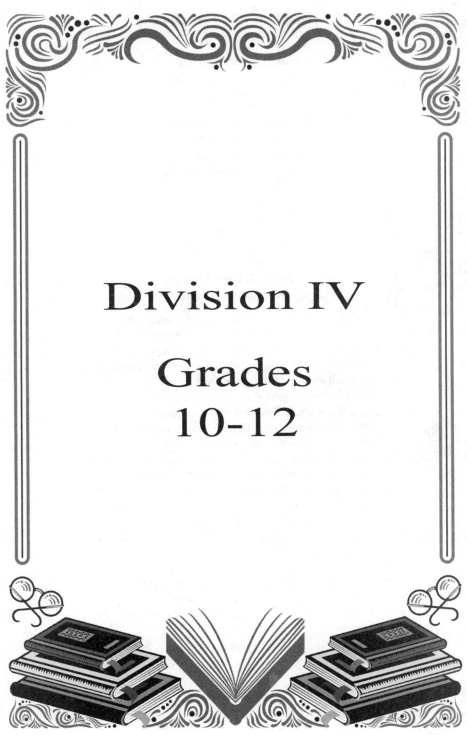

Division IV

Grades 10-12

Flying South For the Winter
by Veronica Kriegl

With the quiet tip-tapping
Of tiny fingers on the trumpet.
I am home,
Once more.
Sitting alongside my mother
And her children.
As if a simple gosling, all over again.
But I am no more a gosling,
Than I am a goose.
Just a wanderer,
Who has found her way–
Back home.

Just Before Dawn
by Amanda Wagner

The metal burns in my fingers, leaving scars,
Scars as deep as the guilt that runs through my body.
I close my eyes, and see the faces of everyone, everyone but ours.
I can't bear the pain, agony, absorbing my thoughts.
We should not be the ones behind bars.
The metal is shiny, blinding my eyes,
Though it is a relief that I cannot see your face or mine.
We are the same, even though we are far from allies.
How come you're so calm?
In a few minutes, we shall prepare to say our goodbyes.
The metal is smooth upon my fingers,
Reflecting the faces that haunt my past and disrupt my future.
Don't interfere with my path. I know what lingers.
My fate is not in your hands,
Even though I hold on to your fate, within my fingers.
The metal now stares you in the face,
And I pull the silent trigger.
This image of you falling, I must erase.
Goodbye, Elisha, goodbye.
You and I no longer remain alive in this space.

A Bouquet of Lives
by Melissa Ryan

A gift for a job well done.
Flowers are given. A bouquet won.
But from whom were they taken away?
The birds? The bugs? The butterflies? The skies of blue and gray?
The doe who needs strength to bear her child.
The other deer, rabbits, and furry friends running wild.
The bee, needing nectar to do work for the queen,
Returns for more, but not one single flower is left to be seen.
This palace of color, and soft, cotton walls,
Was ripped from the ground, stems, roots, and all.
Leaving room for rain, without roots to clean up.
Allowing slugs to appear for the sun to dry up.
The shade is gone from the ground. The cover is lifted.
Only species allowed are the ones who are gifted:
The fish and frogs inhabit the lake.
The bunnies rest, never to awake.
What once was a field has filled up with water.
Think about this next time you give flowers to your daughter.

Change: After Gail Mazur
by Lauren Del Turco

The old woman that wobbles around the park, too,
Staring at the broken picture he left on the doorstep,
Has kissed endless prayer beads and prayed with no end
For a chance to go back; for a chance to try again.
These last optimistic weeks before dead winter,
I search for cause to have hope, to smile.
The golden tinge to his eyes, which glows,
Is nothing more than a color, a cover
For the person (I know) he'd never be,
Though who I somehow still need–and still search for–
Like the red glow of his brake lights
While I stand in the road with wet eyes
And frostbitten fingers, that reach fraily for the heart,
Now lying mangled beneath the slowly falling snow.

Dear Barbie
by Molly Klemarczyk

You know, for three years straight
That life-size Barbie doll was the first thing
On every one of my birthday, Christmas, just-because-you-love-me lists.
But now, I'm glad that it never showed.
Six-year-old me would've never guessed I would've met you one day!
A real, truly there life-size Barbie doll.
So here it is, Barbie,
Now that I've known you for a while,
I've dedicated a verse or two
To you, and every girl who ever looked
Like a super model and a mannequin at the same time.
Who made me believe that blondes do have more fun
And brown was mediocre.
To every girl who sighed out their self-esteem when you walked by
And dreamt of plastic-smooth skin along with a microscopic shoe size.
So sorry, Barbie
I've crossed you off my Christmas list.
And, no–I don't really want to meet Ken.

Random Thoughts
by Victoria Roeck

Dinner last night
A bowl of steaming hot chicken soup
What I bought at the mall
A flowing green shirt
What happened at the zoo when I was three
I tried to straighten the spiraling tail of a pig
What I watched on TV this morning
A rerun of Boy Meets World from 1998
My birthday present
A diamond shaped silver pendant necklace
The homework I haven't done yet, and could've been doing now
My confirmation class that my mother teaches
The house I live in
The friends I have
And what life would've been like without me

Victoria
by Sara Vaclavik

The drone of your tone rumbles a moan
From my throat to your own, even as we cry across the telephone wire
Sire, fire your mind and risk your heart,
And I won't start on the politics of love
Forgive me, please; drink your wine and free the dove,
And I'll unglove a hand crystal-bright and virgin-white
To touch you in the exhausted light of night
Eye the sight, scream in fight, or fright–
One has your baritoned throat in clutches
And much as I want to rescue you ... I can't.
I'm too much a madame, too far a delicacy for men's lips as their hips crawl
Along sheets stiff and starched, stiff and starched–
And they leave me to march in their wretched processions–
Oh, oppressions and depressions of a damsel
As she lies lonely in the home, alone, alone, and reaches for a telephone
Sounding a tone stiff and starched, stiff and starched ...

The Somnambulist
by Shawn Ahmad

Was it kismet, was it fate, that we would come to meet
On a day in which stars would unite and coalesce?
I recall how easily our passions came to greet,
How easily my fingers came to acquiesce
To the golden meadows of thy luscious hair.
I reminisce how eagerly I embraced thee with a running start,
With the desire to stop time and feel the beatings we still share,
Received from the relentless pulsation of the human heart.
But lately events became parlous, precarious, so perilous;
You begin to eschew me, to push me aside;
Your love is becoming inauspicious, so injurious.
Like a clairvoyant I've a premonition: it shows that you've died.
Like a child, I remain steadfast and continue to adore;
Awake all night, yearning for what has died forevermore.

The Wrong Binder
by Kimberly Abruzzo

Dear my long lost paper,
I remember the night when I slipped you into one of my binders.
And I remember the night I placed that binder into my black backpack,
Safe and sound.
I remember when I opened a binder to find you gone.
All the time we spent together now seems like a waste.
All the thought I put into you is now gone.
Now, I have a grade much lower than you would have been.
And because of your absence, I have to rewrite a five page paper
On a topic I don't even understand, using sources I can't even read.
And it's all because I actually just put you in the wrong binder.

Greetings, My Name Is Sally
by Teresa Mason

Greetings, my name is Sally.
No wait, Sandy.
Or maybe it's Sandra.
Who knows
But the one who gave
The essential name to my being?
What does it matter
What is on legal papers?
I feel like my name should be ...
Betty.
Or Barbara. Yes. I like Barbara.
Betty is more practical than Sally.
Sally just reminds me of silliness.
I am more practical than silly.
My name suits me now.
And now I can live the life Sally couldn't
But the life Betty will.

School Equals Drama Part II
by Lyndsay Tricarico

School is filled with drama
There's rumors, fights, and lies
Everybody starts it
But more so girls than guys
So word by word and punch by punch
Each person spreads a rumor
For the victim they get mad
While others think it's humor
Some don't really realize
The trauma that they cause
When they say such hurtful things
And point out all your flaws
But if we stand up for what is right
And help those who are in pain
Then we can make a difference
And stop this hurtful chain

The Cry of the Soldiers
by Shivonne Hancock

Long ago, a shadow fell over the battlefields of Gettysburg.
North against south; brother against brother
It was the shadow of death.
As I walked on those same fields, the tears came to my eyes.
I can feel their pain, and I can hear their cries.
So many wounded, missing, or gone
Stones in lines, with numbers, names unknown.
Where the Blue and Grey find common ground
How many thousands died on this ground, where I stand?
This land before me is holy
These fields remain untouched since 1863 to honor these men
As the cold wind blows against my back
I see the shadow again, and, in the sunset, I cry.

Don't Take It the Wrong Way
by Aaron Ocasio

Don't take it the wrong way,
I'm just sayin',
This is true love; this ain't for playin'.
This is my life, and I want ya to stay in.
I know we been through it, and got our months and days in,
But I want us to be together, even after our days end.
Yeah, I'm kinda clever with my words;
Not even talking about the bees and the birds!
Now forget about the nouns and the verbs,
Baby, I just hope that I'm being heard!
Don't take it the wrong way; I was just mad
Because I never experienced something like what we had
For you to be with me, I'm just glad;
Even happier times when our kids call us Mom and Dad.

The Other Me
by Danielle Koebli

I watch myself walk away,
Into another world, another place.
She is me, and I am her,
My other half, as I am hers.
I live in a place of normality
Her world is filled with demons and destruction,
Of gifts and betrayal.
She works for anyone, yet only herself,
She believes in nothing, but trusts love.
She is my opposite, my other half.
She is me, upside down and backwards.
When I look into her eyes, I see what I wish to be.
She wishes to trade places, to trade pain.
I would switch in an instant, to be who I really am.
I would gladly trade if it could be real.
I know who she is, and she, I.
She is my other half.
And as I wave goodbye, as she goes down her path,
I wave goodbye to me, the one I wish to be.

Unwritten
by Amanda Nee

I wait at the starting line.
Bow pair taps at our coxswain's command.
We all act on her word,
We can't imagine any other choice we have.
Seat three whispers in my ear,
Let's win this war. She pronounces each syllable.
I reach back and pound her fist, like always.
Her eyes burn, and ignite mine.
Sit ready all boats, bellows the official
Who has clearly been in the sun too long.
It is setting now, blinding and burning.
I close my left eye to regain sight.
It may be hours now
Since my bare toes scrunched the grass,
When the dull hum of Coach's words
Fought for our furious minds' attention and lost.
My girls are sitting behind me;
Seats three, two, one, cox.
Tears and regret I've known all too well.
I grip harder. Knees slam down. Pull like hell.

Ode To My Parents
by Brittany Mahachek

Oh parents, how you annoy me with your chores
And how you make me do my homework before I can go out
But I know it's because you care
And you want the best for me
And I know sometimes I make you mad
With acting goofy and not listening to you
But it's because I care
And I like to annoy you
You always make my day better
With a joke or something funny
And I know I can always come to you
Because you are the best listeners
Oh parents
I know when you tell me to wear a helmet
It's not so that I am the only 16 year old with a helmet
It's only because you don't want me to get hurt
Oh parents, I love you

Green
by Rebecca Cardenas

Lost in a forest of mystery and wisdom,
Giant pines form a path among the night,
Bright mint earth at my feet,
The fresh scent overwhelms my senses.
Suddenly, I'm at port.
Soldiers dressed in their uniforms march in line across the field.
Clair de Lune plays iridescently from under the boardwalk
Where green scaled mermaids flap their unsullied fins.
The horseshoe necklace around my neck breaks
And falls onto the wet, freshly cut grass.
The Buddha's jade beads, wrapped around his wrist,
Protect him from the wars of mankind.
Emerald city gates beckon the possibility of peace,
Summon the taste of sushi wrapped in seaweed melting in your mouth,
The sting of parsley recalls the memory of my old pea coat.
Found in a palace of palm trees swaying in the zephyr.

Baseball Team
by Rathin Pathak

Every game we hear the boos
Every game we tend to lose
But we look nice and neat, like Mr. Clean
When we bat, we miss the seams
And as a tailor who does not know how to sew
We still keep trying
Coach keeps buying bats
Before we start, we have a plan
But we always end up sitting on our hands.
We keep our eye on the ball
Hoping to hit it high in the sky
The bat talking to us like, "You suck."
We just don't have good luck.
So ding! Another hit from the other team
But we will balance out like the beam.

Why Sun?
by Michael J. Wieczenski

Sun may live, sun may die; it seems so close to life
Like the sunrise and the sunset.
It's like all stars shining, beginning to booming end.
The enjoyments, the pleasures, and the failures
And why shine? Why shine now?
When the sun may shine never.
The sun would never feel a pleasure, or feel a failure.
Stars may gleam brighter than the sun, it seems.
So, why, sun? Why burn your fuels as bright as they do?
Why are you just as bright in the dawn as you are at dusk?
Why do you not burn all your fuels away?
That way, you may be infinite.
That way, you may never feel pain.
And all failure would be forgotten.
Then, the sun would be brighter than any star ever seen.
And your gleam would only be seen in the dreams of young stars.
I ask why, sun, do you burn the way you do?
It's only in my dreams, the day your sunset comes.

Wanted
by Josh Martin

We are the puppets in the closet
We sit in our tomb, as we take pride in our strings
Thriving on our pasts, with faith in the future.
We are sturdy. We are strong.
We are not afraid of the dark.
We do not sit in fear.
We are not influenced by the lack of light, but we will promise.
We will promise you something, as sure as your shadow in the sun
That we will be triumphant, we will see the light ...
And we will be wanted.

Her
by Renan Delima

Her smile brightens my day like the sun
Her eyes are two bright stars
Her lips kiss me gently in the sunlight
Her heart helps me smile when I'm feeling down.
Her life is mine and my heart is hers
Her love hits me with strong force
Her happiness brings a smile to my face
Her care makes me feel special.
Her trust shows her faithfulness
Her beauty drives me crazy.

Crush
by Christina Navarro

Every time I talk to you, "Chitter, chitter, chat,"
I lose my breath, and can't find the words.
I get so nervous and shy,
I turn as red as a rose.
I am so anxious to see you,
And hear you talk,
My gut is a butterfly.
I feel like I am spinning and my gut is going to burst.
I can't help but act stupid, or stutter, or stumble around you.
This feeling is telling me this could be more than a crush.

When We Date
by Peter W. Coll

When we both agree to begin
Hallelujah, Christ is within
Everything shall be for His win
No hidden love, no secret sin
We will be in truth, and in light
Even our love is in plain sight
Deemed good by our parents, God will
Approve. Till God's will we fulfill
Take my hand, look upon that hill
Embracing that cross is our will

Poems Get Me In Trouble
by Miles Pastrof

I hate poems with a passion.
It's just as dreadful as school.
My teacher keeps yelling at me,
Because I'm taking so long to write this.
She gave me the whole weekend to write it.
But I decided not to try it.
I'm as dumb as Kevin, my other friend,
Who decided not to write it.
This is the end.
I don't know what else to write.
So I'm going to hand it in
With confidence and pride.
"Ring, ring," my heart is ringing,
School is over and my heart stops beating.

Growing Up
by Hugo Galindo

He lost his heart,
The day his girl left.
He lost his hands,
The day his best friend left.
He became a ghost,
The day he moved.
It's not Kevin, Chris, or James.
It's you, it's me, it's everyone

One Symbol
by Nicholas Sertich

A symbol of hope,
A sight of love;
A show of majesty,
A haven of life;
A home of liberty,
A gathering of faith;
We are one nation,
One symbol of our strength.

Nine Months
by Rikki Lauzon

Sitting across from you, seeing me stare,
You pass me in the hallway,
No sympathy, because you don't care.
You got what you wanted from me,
Something that will never be taken back.
As you tell your friends,
My faith is hacked,
By the fact there won't be any of the word "us".
I hear the sound of a crack.
Only nine more months to go, to show what we did.
Look at our mistake; now we really can't take it back.
Ignore me as you please,
But in the next nine months
There's going to be another one of you or me.

My Comet
by Lizzy Marin

Broken hearted you took me
And broken hearted you fixed me
You made me happy to have you by my side
Happy that I was never hurt inside
Like a piano you became the key to my tune
Happy you made me, that I want to marry you soon
Happy you made me, that I choose you to lay next to my tomb
You make me joyful, you bring love to reach millions of miles
Your like a comet, flying in the sky
Your the reason of my happiness
Your the reason I can fly
O big comet, Take me out to the milky way again
O big comet, I want to dance with you again
It's now time for me to go off bed
Thank you for fixing my broken heart again
Goodnight, into tomorrow
Have a good sleep and see you same time tomorrow
I will look out from my window and see you again
Keep me save my little comet, old friend

Papayas
by Catherine Verdic

I pluck the papaya from the tree,
I took away its innocence,
It may be harder for it to grow,
But I think the tree will manage to survive,
With a lot of tender, loving care.
In my kitchen, I put pressure on the fruit,
To find the mushy spots.
I drive the knife through its soul,
The juice spills down its sides,
Like a waterfall.
In my garden; I replant the seeds.
A glowing tree will protect the papayas,
But not now, this papaya is far too young,
But one day.

Mary
by Mary Borowiec

Sea of bitterness
Japan flowering cherry
Like Mother Mary
Quite contrary

A Rebel's Declaration
by Paige Cannon

Let's take a ride
Away from the good of the world
Let's walk along side death and devastation
Sit on the borders of Hell
Dangle our feet over its pits of fire
Let's pretend to hate evil
Kiss difficulty on the cheek, and flirt with mistake
Let's push our limits
Who wants it easy anyway?

If Only They Knew
by Heather Saurel

They say beauty is on the inside and out
A theory not always true
There's something about it that fills me with doubt
If only they knew!
You have a good character, nice and sweet
But you don't have any friends, not even a few
You're always made fun of by everyone you meet
If only they knew!
Sitting next to the window, still wondering, "Why?"
Staring at the sky that's bright and blue
Not seeing the difference they see at times
If only they knew!
They can't see the hurt I have inside
From the pain they put me through
So, I run away and hide
If only they knew!
If only they knew
And saw from my point of view
Too bad they don't even have a clue
If only they knew!

Ancestry
by Monica Oliveira

Oliviera, "Olive tree."
Bounded by the roots that connect us,
But I don't have the same last name.
I don't know the name of my grandfather.
For years, my mother and I
Have walked the streets.
I look into the faces of men,
Who resemble the face of my mother.
Curl here, tendril there,
Abundant on the head of my mother and brother.
Do you have curls on your head
Grandfather?
Ribeiro, "Riverbank."
Just as water nourishes humanity,
My family nourishes me.
Do you have any memories of my mother,
Grandfather?

My Guitar
by Jonathan Chavarry

My guitar is a beast running through the hills,
Like a plow through fields,
His bellow being heard beyond the horizon,
Like the earthquake under our feet.
My guitar is like the chill you get at night.
He is like sand and stone.
He can put you to sleep.
He can beat you into misery.
His presence will signify greatness.
His strings moving like the waves of the sea.
His sound as brutal as a boulder, symbolizing pure power.
He resembles a god.
He will be cared for, driving imitators to flee from him.
All who play his brothers will respect his purpose.
He will carry us all to greatness.
This instrument is a masterpiece of life.
It is a symbol of life.

The Slave of Sin
by Anthony Baglio

A lost man without control,
A captive of his burning soul,
He doesn't talk and doesn't cry,
He holds his emotions deep inside.
A blind man cannot stand,
Within his castle made of sand.
Tornadoes of confusion cloud his brain,
He fights his sickness, but can't abstain.
A slave of sin, a prisoner who dwells,
In the dark dungeon, the abyss of hell.
The devil tempts him both day and night,
Curled up in a corner devoid of light.
A mind of lust is a dangerous disease,
An evil magician with an expertise.
Kill your addiction and ease the pain,
Move past the friction and you will gain.
Hold on tight and run from Hell,
Let the power of the Lord Christ impel.

Caterpillars
by Mia S. Boxer

Childish play preserves the heart.
In meadows dancing, connecting the stars
A spoiled heart expires, unable to restart.
Simplicity becomes anger, bitter and harsh,
Because anger is simple. Search for caterpillars
To name. Childish play preserves the heart.
Make melodies that do not upset the strings of a harp.
Each dagger, every word, leaves a distinct scar.
This is why a spoiled heart expires, unable to restart.
Wilting leaves give in, and drift to the earth.
Minutes fall from the clock, reminding each aged pore,
That childish play would have preserved the heart.
Molds smother the pure part, now it starves.
An apple fades, a foul cloud engulfs the strong cheddar,
A spoiled heart is expired, and unable to restart.
Chase fireflies that feverishly long to depart.
Trust the words of those who ache in rocking chairs.
Childish play preserves the heart.
A spoiled heart expires, refusing to restart

Little Girl
by Yasmine Massac

Little girl in third grade
Yes, I was afraid
New friends, new school
A whole new set of rules
"Terrorists!" blasted all the radio stations
Fingers pointing every which way across the nation
That was the year that my life changed
Ashamed and confused and consumed by rage
Little girl: Yes, that's me
Black and beautiful and Muslim, I be
I'm not a terrorist
I'm not afraid to share this
Little girl is not ashamed anymore
Tell everyone I bring peace, not war
You be who you are and I'll be me, too
As-Salaam-Alaikum, peace be unto to you.

A Hummingbird's Horizon
by Joseph McMahon

In my creaking vessel, over whip-cracking waves, I am rowing out to sea.
On the shore, stands one lone, dark figure,
Arms waving just behind the waves' foaming tongue-tips,
As if wary of being devoured. I row once, hard.
The horizon, the blazing eternal gateway, like some tryst between Heaven and here.
I row once, hard.
Water's luscious lips kiss my ankles, caressing me, numbing me.
"To the horizon, to the horizon." I row once, hard.
Water's luscious lips have reached my knees.
The horizon, that blazing gateway, where solace is wrought of pink hues.
Water's lips caress me. I take my plunge.
I slip, dive seamlessly with an empty shore as my landscape.
I pedal the water, the ocean.
I flap, flutter my arms, water's eager lips almost meeting mine.
The horizon, that blazing eternal gateway.
I pedal harder, and harder, I flap my arms, my wings, as a gull fights the wind.
The horizon, my blazing eternal solace.
The hummingbird beating her wings a hundred times a second,
Just to keep her head still.
The horizon, God's gateway, wrought of hope.
I stop my cyclist's feet, my waving arms, my hummingbird wings.
I never saw the horizon

Jasmine
by Josselyn Rodriguez

As the wind blows through me, it's like your golden fur caressing my skin.
Your excitement as I walked through the door is another smile put in my heart.
Now, life lays low as you become part of the stars.
My spirit begins to fall, knowing that I couldn't do anything to save you ...
So my spirit walked away from me.
"Tick, tock," time passes by, yet the pain doesn't get any softer,
And the guilt can't get any deeper.
The gate for you opens and now I know I'm really late.
That's when the moon fades.
There will be days where I'll look up and smile, because I love you;
Days where I'll stop and miss you, because I'm remembering you;
And days like this one, where I'm staring at your picture and tear because I had you–
I once had you!

Marines
by Matthew Rouwendal

We will march together
We will stay forever
We will fight with death before dishonor
As Marines we will be able to endure
Because this is the code of our brotherhood
Everyone will be sad when we're gone for good

The Box
by Jamie Wilson

I held the ticking box in hand,
The grasping of a grain of sand.
If only I could break the tape,
To move ahead from lonesome state.
The box was shut, to my dismay,
But time passed on, though locked away.
A factor out of my control,
The ticking I could not annul.
To find a place among the rungs,
Of many living, breathing lungs.
Struggle not for breath, but for a place,
In this society's fast pace.
I leave the box to tick away,
A clock cannot hold me at bay.
To move ahead without constraint,
A life of joy I will acquaint.

Rain
by Tajahona Francis

I love the rain
The rain is like the emotions of the world
It's a time when everyone's hardships are the same, when everyone is in unity
The rain understands and cries with us
And when it's done ...
The sun comes out ...
And hope shows its face ...
And pain is slightly melted away ...

Amber Glow
by Wesley Mincin

Red and yellow painted leaves
Hang idly within the trees
They break and sail along the breeze
As fires of autumn's time
They dance and surf upon the ground
Overlap each other with ruffling sound
A setting I am glad I found
As fires of autumn's time
Like fires of the autumn season
They leap and dance without a reason
A factor of autumns many seasons
As fires of autumn's time
The grey clouds break, the sun appears
The dancing leaves appear to sere
These flames it's kept for many years
As fires of autumn's time

The One
by Mecca McDonald

I'm on this mission once again, looking for the one.
I've been here before discarding the clichés that always end the same.
Lies,
Cheating,
Forbidden loves,
Friends turned soul mates,
Tears,
Heartbreak.
It always ends the same!
Yet craving mystery, adventure, and epic journeys brings me back to this
Dusty,
Stone walled,
Literary world.
To take the plunge for a story that has yet to be read or lived.
Praying for the best
I reach out
Take a deep breath
And pick a new book.
Knowing it might be the one.

Evening Dawn
by Jacqueline Mohen

Dusk that plagues the sky with its exhilarating color scheme,
Camouflages the landscape, objects now not what they seem.
Shadows, ever-present in light, grow stronger once the time is right.
The distant "whoo" alerts me of the passing of another day,
Announced by the dusk's rooster
As it focuses its attention on the first unsuspecting critter that scampers by.
Crimson and tangerine are swallowed whole
By the lustrous cloak of sudden darkness, embellished with flickers of white gold.
Thunder roars, nearly snapping its harness.
The shrieks of lightning fill my spirit with delight.
The show has begun.
Wild with energy, spontaneous, angry, with an unquenchable thirst for bark.
A tree split in two.
Every passing moment, another ethereal movement is executed.
I become completely entranced by the tango of flashing bolts
With the gruff, yet sensuous, groan of thunder, until intermission clears the floor.
The curtain, an austere smokescreen, stifles my viewing pleasure
And invokes the postponed essence of deep slumber
Hiding behind my occupation with nature's most captivating performance as of yet.
Unfortunately, I will not witness the second half.

Opportunity Knocks
by Meghan DiMartino

Life is nothing more
Than a series of door after door.
Opportunity knocks once or twice,
Open the door and roll the dice.
They will be there to close one door,
But when they do just open one more.
Of course, they won't want you to succeed,
But keep on striving make being successful a need.
All of you have set goals, and have achieved.
Know that after your hard work you feel relieved.
Don't let them tell you that you're not good enough
Because when it comes down to it
You win though your journey was very rough.

Goodbye, My Love
by Tyler Coltelli

At night, I sit alone, in pain
Just hoping I don't have to hit that vein
To be by myself and have to think
Having my heart just always sink
Committing all seven sins
Deprived me of who I could have been
Now, if only I had listened to my friend Luke
I wouldn't have always had to puke
While looking up to my brother
Never realizing that I always hurt my mother
Now, everyday, as I try to stay clean
I pray that life won't be too mean
So I hope I never go back
To my old self that would shoot up smack
As I hope, one day, to become a dove
I now say goodbye, my love

Take the Chance
by Brianna Lewis

Up, down, left, right
North, east, south, west
Never knowing where you will wind up
Flying in and out of tunnels
You swing left, the cart goes right
Starting like a slithering snake at the bottom of a hill
Then, faster and faster, like a cheetah sprinting across the grassland
The anxiety forms inside of you
It creates a swelling feeling in your stomach,
You scream. Everything just stops!
Then, poof! The cart is gone again
Like you just rolled the dice
It's all chance of which side it will land on
Spinning around and around
Having no idea when you will slow down
Down the hill, you see the end
You step out of the cart and explode in excitement
Knowing the thrill of chance.

I Can Hear Your Body Talking
by Kaitlyn Brakel

Open up your mind,
Let me explore your thoughts a little.
Expand your mouth and let me see what you've been hiding.
What is that lying behind your teeth?
A little white lie? Just what I expected.
You thought I'd never see it.
Maybe you figured you had washed your face enough times
To get rid of that guilty smile.
Keep trying, my friend.
It still lingers on your mouth, sliding up to your ears,
Proving me right time after time.
Maybe you should open up your ears too,
Then you will hear how pathetic you sound
When you're flooding me with your apologizes.
You'll tighten your gut as I say I won't accept your cries.
I hope your stomach aches with regret.
Your legs are weak after carrying around the extra weight of lies.
I'm not taking you back this time,
I'm stronger than your toughest line.
I'm standing my ground.
Pick up your feet and walk away,
I'll watch as your body crumbles with every step you take.

Poppy's
by Elizabeth DiPietro

Let the rain fall down and wash you away
I'm so tired inside, I know I can't stay
Let the rain fall down and drown me alive
Because I know I can't win this fight.
There's too much throbbing, too much crying
So tired, so alive
So against the reason to go on
Revitalized, I'm re-energized,
But, now, tainted forever by loss.
Loss, but not lost–a new sense of being
Instilled within me, a new hope.

Unforgettable Love
by Sarah Zwerko

I wanted one of the love stories
You read about in books.
With those infamous first kisses
And those long estranged looks.
With those lines of
'I'll love you forever;'
Those sweet whispers
'We'll always have each other.'
Love like that only happens once.
Every moment you spend together;
Seared in your memory
Through all the tears and laughter.
That's how it was like for me,
The moment your eyes caught mine.
The world seemed to stop.
And the sun finally began to shine.
You became my heroin;
My own personal brand.
Addicted to you and your love
More than you'll understand.

Gathered One and Gathered All
by Karoline Panes

Gathered one and gathered all;
Despite their emotions, they still stood tall.
Words that described his life
Made everyone tear, especially his wife.
His children there so young and naïve.
This event was one hard to believe.
As they lay his body on the ground to sit,
Red and white roses covered his casket.
As more tears began to flow,
There was no where to go, but grow.
His memory will be in everyone's heart,
Although they will be miles apart.
His body will remain over time,
But his soul will always remain near mine.

Tigers
by Michael Homsack

Tigers are vicious creatures that hunt
And kill their prey with their long claws
Scratch!
In the winter they sleep and snore.

The Perfect Wave
by Nick Burdi

There I was, on the beach
Finally, the time had come
As I looked out, the ocean looked as if it had jets from a Jacuzzi
White wash and foam lay on top of the angry sea
Bombs coming in twelve to fifteen feet
Heavy, hollow, spitting, dredging barrels
Roaring as far down the beach as you could see
Offshore winds howling at twenty-five mph
Surfline rated it an epic day
There is no wonder why the conditions were flawless
So amped up, there was no holding me back
I jumped in
The chilling water rushed through my wetsuit
A paddle out that seemed to take forever, was well worth it
Me and one other guy
Waiting for the perfect wave
We saw one rolling in
Looked like a ferocious mountain of water coming straight for me
The guy yelled, "Go, go!"
So I went
Ten feet of water on both sides of me
Trying to suck me into its wrath
So, I started pumping harder
Harder and harder
Yes! I yelled as the wave gave up and spit me out
Looking for the steepest section
I put all my weight into a bottom turn
Flew up the face
And out the back
It seemed as if I was a bird soaring through the sky
Then plop!
Back into the water I went
The perfect ride was done
I paddled back out searching for another one.

Blink
by Madeline Benz

Eighty tiny soldiers line the battlefront
Fifty more reside as reinforcements
Separated by a distance that to them seems large
To you or I seems small ...
Minuscule, not a feat at all.
These warriors guard their castle
Keeping watch on either side
Cautious of unwanted intruders
Prepared to make a necessary glide.
Constantly clashing comrades
Are often overlooked
As they protect this jewel or flower
This shaker or stream
Segway into dreams at the appropriate hour.
Advertised for beauty
And quite successful in this task
Though occasionally providing a mask
Their function is forgotten
As these warriors guard their castle
As these soldiers wait to fight.

Gilded Rubbish
by Amy Plante

All streetlights shall be purple
And illuminate the deer
On the sidewalks
The padlocks
The cornstalks
And the wolf stalks
Lurking at the entrance to the museum
Waiting for Bruno, the street singer
The meat slinger
The beat bringer
A bringer of Daily News
Of new shoes
Of rhythm and blues
And noisy puppets who gather and clutch
The souls of the lost ones
Who'd rather not say much.

Secrets of the Everlasting Earth
by Bethan Johnson

And as I stood there, a wanderer of sorts,
The wind blew me
And the mist engulfed my very essence.
The great grass of old seemed to wave me, guide me onward,
Directing my eyes to hills and rocks.
And upon that crag I stood, silent and patient,
Like the weathered stones beneath me.
In time a quiet swell quaked within me,
My shivers a rhythmic force.
The ruffling grass and howling winds
Carried the ancient songs on their tongues.
Combined they made a symphony around me, a ballad inside me.
And the shivers that erupted from my chest on that crag
Course through me even now.
It is because that day, as nature danced around me,
Celebrating, she whispered the song of the ages,
And it will pulse through me, strong, honest and pure, forever.

When Life Doesn't Look the Same
by Lynda Nguyen

I wake up sometimes, wishing I could remember
What it was like when you were there.
When your smile melted my worries,
When there never was an end.
Remember what it was like when your arms protected me from the rain?
When you'd hug me and not let go?
Now, every day, there's a rainstorm that I can't escape.
Every day, I fall trying to hold onto you.
But you're not there. And I'm alone. Abandoned.
Then I'd try really hard to remember what it was like.
Before yesterday. Before the shot. Before that one mistake ruined us, ruined you.
When you left without a word.
Remember what it was like when I cried over your bag of bones?
When I screamed your name? When my voice was stolen by my misery?
I remember that day.
When I wondered where peace was.
What was peace? What about peace?

Used Granted Wish
by Briana Canavan

This has been too long,
What was once seen as a granted wish, has now come to diminish.
Tears she withholds; the pain of such defeat
Depressed to any stress,
There was never to be any less.
She takes on to another level.
Hopefully to break free from the devil.
The blood that she bleeds only erases her mind for that one moment in time.
She sees her reflection to the cuts she forever will see.
Don't know what to do.
Trying to balance it all,
So she won't hit another mental wall.
She races left to right, seeking for that other side of the mountain.
She's climbing with what may seem to be all she's got left.
Tired of chasing,
No longer want to be misplacing.
She searches to get that betterness.
She's come too far to turn back, so whatever she may lack
She'd better start to see, and start running that track.

I Used To Be Good Enough, Now I'm Just Me
by Jennifer Whitford

There was a time when my mind teemed with dreams,
Childhood ambitions, and fantasies.
Drive bubbled up inside me, and at my seams
I nearly burst from feeling so alive.
Then, high school came, and I was thrown a blow,
Right to my heart it came. For I never knew
My dreams, which were once able to grow
Could be torn, crushed, and then lost forever.
It was you, my dear, who made me feel
As worthless as the bottom of the food chain.
The goal of Princeton dashed from my mind
As surviving freshman year became my main.
You're a shark, but this fish will find her way,
You will not repress me, no, not today.

Struggle To Breathe
by Michael Doughty

I struggle against the hold
Gasping and flailing about
Your hold isn't tight
But I feel myself falling
I can't fight the hands anymore
And I fall limp
I'm still alive, but I feel dead
You let go and I'm alive again
I rub my neck, silently wondering
If the hands were still there
After that battle.

Third of July
by Sara Jansson

My father is exploding with frustration
Like the day-early fireworks overhead.
They blast every car alarm in the 3A section,
Howling in fear that someone is taking them.
I ran my sticky hands down my chubby child legs.
My stomach detests the sick sweetness
Of perfectly pure and innocent cotton candy,
Too bad I ate it all.
Up high enough to see
The L-I-double-R shot out of its barrel,
Immigrants lurking on bicycles under the overpass,
The vampire bats over Shea Stadium.

Forever Taken
by Jess Pauciello

She woke up with the biggest smile on her face
Now isn't that out of place?
As typical as arsenic and lace.
Who managed through, through that unbreakable wall?
It was the boy who came yelling with the call:
"I'll always catch you if you fall!"
This Jersey girl, her feelings she isn't faking.
This time, her heart will not be breaking
It's safe with him; she's forever taken.

Call of Gravity
by Michelle Bayman

The tree bleeds,
The liquid trickles over jagged bark
Seeps into cracks and rolls over mold
Blurring both into a dark brown-black hue
Resembling a quintessential broken record;
It leaps over every bump and every knot joyfully
Succumbing to the flirtatious call of gravity,
Hurtling towards the dank ground–
The light glows bright through more obscure clouds
And the birds take up their evening gossip again:
The rain is speechless.

Negative Place Toward To Change Positive Place
by Leah Murray

I walked into the dark place that I hate
I was panicked as I can't find the way
Start running around and screaming for help
But nobody is there, the place is full of echoes
I notice flowers, trees, everything is destroyed; there are storms.
I knew it was gonna happen.
I will be crazy if I'm stuck in the dark place, which is called Negative Place.
I feel I'm already so weak, and I should give up to everything.
I stopped running, heavily panting, and start crying; I'm scared.
I walked carefully because I can't see,
It's very dark; I don't want to fall or get hurt by things
I talk to myself to say, "Please get me out of Negative Place."
Suddenly, I felt so cold, shivering
I have no coat or jacket. I rubbed my arms for warmth
Stopped walking, looked around. I felt that no one would find me.
So I sit down on the ground and still cried.
I feel something strange in this place, a light glowing,
I turn around; there! A door behind me.
I walk toward to the door. I opened the door and went inside the other place.
I notice everything is not destroyed, there no storms, I feel nothing.
I feel so strong and I realized I did not need to give up to everything
I'm happy and free from the dark place. I found the way.

Human Intervention
by Diana Park

The array of bright oranges and yellows
And deep reds lie on the ground
These autumn leaves are altruistic,
Forming a comfortable blanket over the hard floor
And encouraging the others still hanging on for dear life
To stop fearing and to take the final jump
But then here comes father with his menacing leaf blower
The leaves are powerless and scatter in different directions
Stop father!
Don't you see that they need each other?
Look what you have done now
You have interfered with nature once again
And the leaves still hanging on the branches
Tremble in fear

Arise
by Lauren Borromeo

You were meant for greatness
Crumble not in the face of others
As you grow, let the barriers fall with the dust
Do not allow your insecurities to define your self-image
Never let them chip away at your dreams
May the flame in your soul never die
Do not let tragedy be the reason for your downfall
Use the sadness from your past and create the art that is your future
Rise beyond to find the strength you never thought you had
Fly against the clouds that cover your dreams
Break all walls that block your shining light
Let the sound of your laughter forever be part of the music of your life
Do not be afraid
Let the light touch your heart, your very soul
Reach
Embrace the unknown
Free fall and let the wind and your own power carry you
Fear not to fall
Fear not to rise
Only fear the unlived

Free Soul
by Meghan Adkins

I don't want to be locked in a cage
Let me go free
I won't lock up my bonds
If people want to leave they should
I don't want to chain myself to someone forever
I'm a free soul, wandering through the sky of life
I've always lived in wild chaos
And that's how I learned to create
I won't fall in love
My heart belongs to my soul
I'm bound for endless freedom
My love belongs to to the sky
I am the eagle
That guides the country
On a steady course
Fierce, tough, brave, free ...
Alone with a purpose
A leader in the sky
My wingspan protects all
I am the eagle, I am America

Parent's Love
by JaeIn Baek

No matter what children think about their parents,
They say, they work hard as bees for their children,
But I say parents make everything look easy.
They say they do not regret spending their lives on their children,
But this doesn't affect me, because I think they have to do it.
I eat their heart out with anxiety and say stinging words,
They never cry loudly, but
They hold their breath and bathe in tears as pure as pearls.
They say, their children give them pain
But they change pain to love
And it makes the gift to their children as shiny pearl and bright sun,
And I say, now I understand their heart.
Still they say, I am their heart
I elevate them to Heaven or drop them down to Hell.
I know and feel their abundant love,
Their hands protect me from darkness and find the silver lining in the dark,
They lift hope in my heart on birds' wings.
They say, they love their children more than themselves.
So I say, today, tomorrow and every day, I fall in love with my parents.

Living
by Jessica LoGreco

Lying in dead, faded white
Bed sheets.
My face is bruised and grotesquely
Damaged.
Wearing dirty, worn out
Clothing.
Matching perfectly with the lifeless
Flowers.
In the half cracked
Vase.

Struggle
by Chelsea Osuji

I live a life my brothers and sisters are unaware of.
An untold story. An unread book.
They don't know me. No one does.
Who I was. Who I've been. What I've become.
No one sees how I've struggled nor how I worry about my future.
I am a jailbird. Destiny my capture.
I was foolish. Foolish to think I was more than worthless.
Foolish to think that I could be freed from what I'll always be.
What will become of me?
I'm not like others. Intelligent and accepted.
I'm expected to match their perfection.
Walk in their lit path through the darkness.
Instead I chose my own road.
I choose uniqueness and the freedom to be me. I deserve a chance.
A chance to live free of this suffering. Free. Free like a bird.
I live where there's no average, no mistakes, no second chances.
Only perfection and the one try it takes to get there.
I'm Nigerian not American.
I've said it all without saying a word.
The words engraved on this page act as my voice.

Mortal
by Carl Phillips

A beached whale
Lies complacent,
Purple, with golden moonlight
On white sands
As the black ocean
Churns with
Chaotic waves
And turns to ice.

Help
by Emily Drummond

Highway sixty-four. It's raining, pouring.
Through swirling torrents, I spot one lone man.
He's standing, right on the edge of the bridge.
I stop my car, and shout, "hey!" He turns slow.
"Rainy day, no?"
A few moments later,
And he is in my car, talking about his life.
His wife
Died. His daughter,
Deathly ill,
No wonder.
"I want to end it all,"
He stated, "Nobody listens to me."
"I am," I said.
He smiled, clouds parted.
The sun came out of hiding, graced us.
"There's always the next day, make it better." I told him.
He would have died that day,
If I didn't involve myself, if I didn't care.

Dinner In Capetown
by Michele Seabrook

Please they don't even mean anything
The grass is in my mouth and I like it there
And I beg silently from the car only less than 50 feet away,
There you are and the right part of the song comes on
And the canons explode and across the world.
Someone in India has just died and their granddaughter is crying
And in Capetown people are eating dinner
And here I am sitting just being so selfish and petty and pained
And I see the flash of white on the front of your shirt
And I see the other days flash before me
And the other ones and the girls and the tigers and the everlasting cage
And the shame of failing a test and the shame of caring about inanity
And the desire for you yes you,
Do you simply not know what to do with me
Or do I really illicit such indifference in only you in only you,
Please just gallop, the horses watch the people
And the Medieval towns become filled with insanity
And the Black Plague and World War I
Justify it all and allow me to sleep at night knowing there is no God.

Is It Me
by Shakimah Kates

Is it me, the smile I have on my face
The joy I have in my soul
The love I have in my heart
That just turned into gold.
Who is it, the pain I once told
The fear I had that lived deep down in my soul.
What is it, the shame that roomed my mind
The shadow that beat me from behind
"How could it" How could it be
Me, now I'm so free and happy.
"Why should I" Why should I look back
I just realized it's Dee
The beloved diva, who is telling this story

A Sliver
by Jenna Intersimone

Even with all that happened
The only thought that remains
Is how much I regret
Not slow dancing with you in the parking lot
That quiet night in November

Calypso's Sorrow
by Adam Sands

Why do those undying gods
Always take what is not theirs?
They do what they will
Unmindful of the wants, the needs,
Of their very own sister.
They brought that wandering man,
That man of suffering,
Nothing but grief and pain.
Then they brought him to me,
Floating in the salty sea.
I nurtured him, made him whole once more,
I made his physical suffering disappear
I fed him, housed him, and loved him.
I gave him all the time in the world and for what,
So that they can come and take him away?
He is alive due to me
With no help from those gods
Or that brute, Poseidon.
What right do they have to take him,
What gives them the right when I love him?

3rd Place

Ellie Riedel

Ellie is a member of her high school's
Forensics Speech and Debate team.
She has written a lot of poetry over the past year,
and wrote "Split Personality" as a sophomore in chemistry class.
Thanks for sharing it Ellie.
It's one of our favorites!

Split Personality
by Ellie Riedel

A bowed head
A small voiced question
Brown eyes look up
Through black lashes
And take my breath away
Instantly I wish
His question wasn't as innocent as,
"Are you going to art club today? You should ..."
Then he's back to his fun self
Skinny Jeans
Bicolor hair
Tight bright shirt
Loud, bold, obnoxious
They are the two sides
Of this one boy
He walks away from me
Leaving me with green eyes trained on his tall thin form
As his Converse squeak in the hall of normality

2nd Place

Ashley Frey

Ashley is an aspiring artist who loves to capture the world
through poetry, drawing, and photography.
She has won awards in all of these endeavors,
as well as in bowling which she lists as her favorite sport.
We congratulate Ashley
on a beautiful and touching poem.

A Balloon For Daddy
by Ashley Frey

The September breeze caresses my cheek
Bringing with it the aroma of moist chocolate cake
And burning candles from behind
The sound of children laughing and playing in the background
Mother and I, away from the excitement of my birthday celebration
The travail of suppressing tears, pain, and love
Formed Mother's beautiful face
As she firmly clasps my little hand inside her warm embrace
A tacit transfer of anxious emotion joins us
Just before I set the balloon free
The papery string slips from my fingers as I let go
The bold red body transcends the cotton clouds
And disappears from view
Destined for the heavens
Like the balloon, I have let go of childish things
Because there is no longer room for pretend in this intimidating world
Now, stray balloons are always echoing that little girl's whisper–
"I love you, Daddy."

Danielle Shpaner

The toughest choice we face each year
is choosing one poem as our grand champion,
and this year was no exception.
So many talented authors,
and yet one always seems to display that little something extra.
Such is the case with Danielle,
who made her online submission while in the twelfth grade.
We are pleased to present our "Editor's Choice Award"
and highest compliments
to the author of "Void and Cracked".

Editor's Choice Award

Void and Cracked
by Danielle Shpaner

I remember opening the medicine cabinet
And finding a white bottle of liquid capsules,
Only to spin around, and catch him, from the corner of my eye
Inhaling the pungent fumes of Cuban cigars
And burning himself with bittersweet vodka.
I remember tip-toeing to my mother's room
And strangling her with my skinny arms,
Beating her with the weight of my head against her breasts.
"What's wrong with Daddy?"
She covered my question with her palm,
As sturdy as the distinct edges of a stop sign,
And flung my tears like a child, plucking petals from a dandelion.
I picked up his glasses one morning
And crushed them into the barren wood of the kitchen table,
Watching specks of white pierce flushed flesh,
And crimson red stain the creases of my palm.
He knelt down next to me,
Gray strands peeping through his haystack of hair,
His eyes the color of the pavement, void and cracked,
And claimed that now he couldn't see.

Index
of
Authors

Index of Authors

Index of Authors

Index of Authors

Index of Authors

Inspired
Price List

Initial Copy 32.95

Additional Copies 24.00

Please Enclose $6 Shipping/Handling Each Order

Check or Money Order Payable to:

The America Library of Poetry
P.O. Box 978
Houlton, Maine 04730

Must specify book title and author

Please Allow 21 Days For Delivery

THE AMERICA
LIBRARY OF POETRY

www.libraryofpoetry.com

Email: generalinquiries@libraryofpoetry.com

Poetry On the Web

See Your Poetry Online!

This is a special honor reserved exclusively for our published poets.
Now that your work has been forever set in print,
why not share it with the world at www.libraryofpoetry.com

At the America Library of Poetry,
our goal is to showcase quality writing in such a way
as to inspire others to broaden their literary horizons,
and we can think of no better way to reach people around the world
than by featuring poetic offerings like yours on our global website.

Since we already have your poem in its published format,
all you need to do is copy the information from the form below on
a separate sheet of paper, and return it with a $6 posting fee.
This will allow us to display your poetry
on the internet for one full year.

Author's Name _____

Poem Title _____

Book Title _____ *Inspired* _____

Mailing Address _____

City _____ State _____ Zip Code _____

E-mail Address _____

Check or Money Order in the amount of $6 payable to:
The America Library of Poetry
P.O. Box 978
Houlton, Maine 04730